GENERAL SERIES 98

The [illegible] and in the [illegible] h Centu[illegible]

A Social Geography

B. I. COLEMAN

The Historical Association
59a Kennington Park Road, London SE11 4JH

Contents

ACKNOWLEDGEMENTS

The illustration on the cover is of St James-the-Less, Westminster, 1858-1861 originally published in *The Builder,* 1861 and reproduced from *Victorian Architecture: Four Studies in Evaluation,* Columbia University Press, 1978.

ISBN 0 85278 233 0 H.A. 9.5-5-80

Printed in Great Britain by Hart-Talbot Printers Ltd., Saffron Walden

Introduction

English society has always displayed a considerable degree of regional and local differentiation, but that feature became more pronounced between the Tudor and the Victorian periods and notably so with respect to religious life. Perhaps no other society with an official church establishment has shown such a degree of religious pluralism as Victorian England. The subject of this pamphlet is the regional and local aspect of this situation. Anglican practice was not spread evenly across the nation. It had a geography which was part of the total social geography. To say this is not to assert that the religious life of the period can be understood entirely in terms of regions and localities, for much of it can be seen equally well as the local manifestation of national movements and developments. The local and the national were not separable in practice, though it is legitimate to try to isolate one of those aspects. Not does this approach entail a crude determinism that discounts the importance of those personalities, movements and doctrines that have bulked large in traditional accounts of nineteenth-century religion. What it does is put them in a necessary perspective by sketching the social geography within which they operated.

The ideal of the Elizabethan religious settlement had been uniformity and conformity. There should be only one faith, that established by law, and the whole population should conform by attending church regularly, receiving communion and performing the appropriate rites de passage. This ideal remained strong into the nineteenth century but had been imperfectly realized even at the start. The roots of failure lay not just in the uneasy compromise underlying the original settlement but also in the limitations and weaknesses of central government and of the ecclesiastical system it authorized, in the character of the society which government and church sought to control, and in the subsequent growth of population and of a more complicated and diversified economy. The old Catholic faith survived in pockets of local strength and in time there developed forms of Protestantism outside the legal establishment.

The eighteenth century saw an increasingly matter-of-fact acceptance of religious laxity and diversity. The legal and communal pressures to religious conformity were relaxing. Though the Toleration Act of 1689 had extended only minimal toleration to Protestant Dissent, its passage seems to have been followed by a decline in Anglican observance. After 1714 government no longer gave the Church unequivocal support, magistrates and churchwardens became more tolerant of religious neglect and deviance, the system of ecclesiastical discipline over the laity withered away, and the laws for conformity became inoperative and in time inoperable. At first this relaxation of Anglican discipline seems to have entailed no corresponding increase in other forms of practice. Indeed the old Dissent was regressing, particularly in rural areas, for much of the century. When, at the century's end, the successes of a new movement, Methodism, combined with threats to political order to inspire Anglican attempts to restore some of the machinery of religious control, their failure showed that the Church had lost for good the aid afforded by legal restriction and sanction, a fact of greater social significance than the celebrated repeal of the civil disabilities of Dissenters and Catholics in 1828–9. People found themselves freer than ever before to neglect the approved worship and to develop alternative forms as and if they chose. What this entailed was a wider variation in levels of religious practice and an increase in regional and local diversity at the expense of national uniformity.

Despite the decline of legal and communal sanctions, certain social pressures to Anglican conformity remained. Some of them may even have been increasing by the early-nineteenth century, but they were uneven in their impact and they probably accentuated rather than hindered the local differentiation of religious cultures. Those pressures were anyway being exerted in a society undergoing remarkable demographic and economic changes. The population of England and Wales nearly trebled in the century to 1851, and urban growth and industrialization were occurring on an unprecedented scale. These developments made the maintenance of Anglican conformity much harder and gave opportunities to rival denominations. Society was becoming harder to control by traditional means, and the implications were serious for a Church establishment geared (and not particularly efficiently at that) to the needs of a largely agrarian society with the population and the settlement patterns of the medieval period and cumbersomely slow in adapting its machinery to a rapidly changing society. Social and economic change did not 'secularize' society so much as break the traditional moulds in which religious practice had been cast. While some forms of religious expression declined, others increased, and the overall pattern became more varied. The acceptance of some form of Christian belief and of the propriety of religious observance remained widespread, personal morality was commonly understood as Christian morality, and the Protestant tradition emphasized such features as the vernacular Bible, preaching, the role of the laity and the centrality of personal salvation, so that scope remained for an upsurge of religion outside the confines of the establishment.

In the century after 1750 potentiality became actuality. Not only did old Dissent and Roman Catholicism enter new phases of growth, but over those survivals of earlier failures of uniformity was imposed a pattern of Methodist support which extended socially, geographically and numerically well beyond the limits of the old Protestant Dissent. According to the figures of the 1851 Census the places of worship outside the Church of England had increased at least three-fold in every registration county between 1801 and 1851. The Church, which had possessed the majority of places in all counties in 1801, retained it in only seven at the later date.[1] At the same time religious practice had become much more fragmented. The Census Report listed thirty-seven denominations and faiths apart from the establishment itself and those unidentifiable meetings grouped as 'isolated congregations'.[2] Just how Anglican practice itself fared over the century is rather hard to establish. One analysis of thirty Oxfordshire parishes shows a decline in numbers of communicants from 1738 to 1800 (though a steep fall only after 1771), a numerical increase but still, when set against population growth, a proportional decline until 1830, and a general quantitative improvement thereafter.[3] But communion figures are not necessarily a reliable index of other kinds of religious performance and the Oxfordshire parishes may not have been typical of the whole country. It is reasonable to assume that there were considerable regional and local variations in religious practice even at the start of that century of change.

The Census of Religious Worship, 1851

The nineteenth-century patterns of Anglican practice and allegiance can be studied through various kinds of evidence, including an assortment of visitation returns, figures for baptisms, confirmations and communicants, the figures for the various forms of marriage after 1837,[4] and the membership statistics and other records of non-Anglican denominations. This study, however, will concentrate on attendances at worship and on the most important body of statistical evidence, that provided by the unique Census of Religious Worship in 1851. Though the utilization of other sorts of evidence may in time illuminate some of the problems that remain in this field, most recent work by historians has focussed on the Census material. Attendance at Sunday worship was generally recognized as a crucial aspect of religious practice and, for the historian, it is a yardstick that permits some sort of comparison between denominations and between localities. There are, of course, problems in straight comparisons. Statistical evidence of the sort used here tells one little about the great range of types of commitment in and towards the established Church which both benefited and suffered more than other denominations from various sorts of token and occasional conformity. There may have been qualitative differences between types of Anglican practice almost as great as those between Anglicanism and other faiths. Another difficulty is that Anglican attendances on any Sunday were probably a smaller proportion of the total Anglican constituency than attendances in other denominations were of theirs. This was one reason why many Churchmen thought the Census to be misleading and called for a Census of profession rather than of attendance to correct the picture.

The methodology for using the Census evidence in both its printed and primary forms has been given considerable attention by historians, as has the reliability of the data. Though the limitations of the latter become clear when small localities like individual parishes are considered, for larger areas (and the Census was the only survey to cover the whole of England and Wales) there is no doubt that it provides a picture that is both generally reliable and extremely revealing.[5] Its date provides a vantage-point for surveying the remarkable developments of the century before and for gauging the pattern of Victorian religion, though of course 1851 was not the end of change. It was, however, near what seems to have been the high point of regional diversity in religious practice before that diversity—and perhaps 'regionalism' itself—began to decline.[6]

The attendance figures of the 1851 Census are presented here in a double form. First there is the index of attendance (IA)—that is, attendances as a percentage of population. The IA can be given for individual denominations, for denominational groupings and for the aggregate of all forms of worship. Then there is the percentage share (PS)—that is, the attendances of one denomination or denominational grouping as a percentage of the aggregate attendances of all denominations. These are the simplest methods of calculation and presentation, though they are not without certain problems. The Census figures represent attendances, not the numbers of people who attended at least once, and considerable differences between the two are possible. Ways of minimizing that problem are more applicable to the MS returns of the Census than to the printed figures used here. What the Census fails to reveal is the extent of multiple attendance across denominational boundaries, the most common form, particularly in certain rural areas, being worship at the parish church in the morning and at a Wesleyan chapel in the afternoon or evening.

Attendances at worship of all kinds on Census Sunday, 30th March, in 1851 totalled 60.8% of the population of England and Wales after corrections had been made for defective returns, the morning accounting for 25.9%, the afternoon for 17.8% and the evening for 17.1%. The corrected figure for Anglican worship was 29.5% (morning 14.2%, afternoon 10.5%, evening 4.8%). The established Church, in other words, accounted for 48.6% of all attendances. Many Churchmen were disturbed by the figures. Even after allowance was made for those like young children, the aged and the sick who could not be expected to attend, it was clear that the country fell lamentably short of the Elizabethan ideal of total conformity. A reasonable estimate would be that the Church attracted about one-quarter of the population to worship that Sunday. About the same number had worshipped outside the Church of England and perhaps half the population had failed to worship anywhere at all. Horace Mann, the official who compiled the statistics and wrote the Census Report, estimated rather speculatively that over five million people out of nearly eighteen million had absented themselves from the forms of worship available and concluded that 'a sadly formidable portion of the English people are habitual neglecters of the public ordinances of religion.'[7] But however much the established Church in particular and Christianity in general fell short of historic aspirations, the modern observer can be impressed by the scale of observance in 1851. A large part of the population had maintained habits of religious practice even if its forms had become bewilderingly diverse. If the most the Church could claim was a slender majority of worshippers, it remained much the largest single denomination with about three-and-a-half times the attendances of the second largest, the Wesleyan Methodist Original Connexion. The Church's attendances were more evenly spread than those of its competitors. Even in Wales, Cornwall and Durham it attracted attendances larger than its separate denominational rivals could attract almost anywhere. By other criteria it looked even more impressive—it conducted 84.9% of marriages in 1851.[8] The Church's performance was testimony to the strength of its social and economic foundations, to the territorial coverage of its parochial system (unmatched by even the sum total of the Methodist sects), to the numbers, distribution and standing of its clergy and also to the strength of custom and convention.

If the Church was now a 'voluntary' institution as far as attendance at worship was concerned it remained much the greatest of such institutions in an increasingly voluntaristic society. It was by pre-voluntaristic standards of uniformity and conformity that the Church was failing, and one lesson of 1851 was that those ideals were now beyond realization.

The Regions

Behind the national figures lay major regional variations. Some parts of the country simply had a greater quantum of religious observance than others. The aggregate IAs of the Census Report's regional 'registration divisions' ranged from 82.6 in the Welsh Counties and 80.0 in the South Midlands to 37.0 in London and 41.9 in the Northern Counties. The Church's own IA showed a slightly larger variation, from 41.3 in the South Midlands to 16.0 in the Welsh Counties and 17.0 in the Northern Counties. The Church's PS was highest in the South-Eastern Counties (64.2) and lowest in the Welsh (19.3) with Yorkshire (35.6) otherwise the worst division. Outside Wales, which was something of a special case, the Church accounted for about two-thirds of attendances in its best counties and around one-third in its worst.[9]

The most obvious feature of the regional pattern that emerges (see the maps pp 20–21) is the contrast between metropolitan England and the periphery. In an Anglican heartland consisting of most of southern England and the South Midlands the Church's IA and PS were almost uniformly high. The fifteen counties with Anglican IAs above 40 were all south of a line drawn from the Severn to the Wash and so were nine of the eleven counties with the highest Anglican PSs. To the North and West were regions where Anglican attendances were much lower and, in many counties, exceeded by those of the non-Anglican denominations. The registration counties with an Anglican IA of 20 or less were Durham (the lowest with 14.4), North Wales, Northumberland, South Wales, Monmouthshire, the West Riding, Lancashire, Cornwall and Cumberland. Much the same counties returned the lowest Anglican PSs. The figures pointed a familiar contrast. Clergymen of genteel and southern origins who were consigned to parishes in the outer provinces came across distinctive and unfamiliar local cultures (one of them compared his experiences in the Cleveland dales to those of a Christian missionary on Charlemagne's Saxon frontier[10]) and their descriptions of the curious and barbaric ways of these provinces constituted a minor literary genre of the period. The other side of the coin was the celebration of the Anglican idyll of southern England, Trollope's Barsetshire, where the Church felt itself to be most secure. Even here the realities could be less than idyllic, but the assumption that the predominantly rural counties of southern England were the Church's strength had considerable justification.

It was not a simple division between North and South or even between the North and the West on the one hand and the South and the East on the other. A more sophisticated regionalization like the Census's 'registration divisions' or Fawcett's eleven 'provinces of England' was needed to do justice to the pattern of religious practice.[11] But individual counties did not always fit a neat regional divison. Westmorland, Rutland and Norfolk were three counties that stood out from their respective regions. The picture changed anyway according to the criterion adopted. A comparison between Maps A and B (pp 20-21) shows the different patterns produced by the Anglican IA and the Anglican PS. In Cumberland the IA was low but the PS well above the national average. The reverse was true in Bedfordshire. There was, in other words, no firm inverse relationship between levels of Anglican practice and levels of Nonconformity. There were zones of high religious performance where both the Church and Nonconformity attracted good attendances and zones of low performance where both were poorly supported. Other patterns would emerge from the aggregate IA and from the figures for particular non-Anglican denominations or denominational groups. Maps showing only registration counties, moreover, can be misleading. No county was completely homogeneous. In Devon, for example, the division between the two main zones of religious performance in the South-West ran across the county which itself consisted of a number of distinguishable sub-regions. But these local complexities do not invalidate the broad regional pattern which no analysis of the period's religious practice can afford to ignore.

Why this regionalization? Part of the answer lay with long-standing factors in the Church's position and performance and the rest with more recent social and economic developments. Many of the Church's problems were far from new. It had probably always been most effective in that metropolitan region of southern England which had been settled and dominated most completely by continental conquerors and assimilated best by the Augustinian, Anglo-Norman and Reformation churches. Outside this region lay areas that had been less easily and thoroughly controlled and had at various times been resistant or unresponsive to the disciplines Court and Canterbury had sought to impose. Here central authority was weak. Distance from the capital and primitive communications had limited the effectiveness of the writ of secular and ecclesiastical authority. Terrain itself was a factor in this regionalization and particularly the concentration of uplands outside the southern counties. Though not as sharp a dichotomy as that between the Scottish Highlands and Lowlands, the division between upland and lowland zones had been a major influence on religious performance and development in England. The Church was strongest in the fertile lowlands that had been heavily settled and prosperous in the medieval period when the parochial structure had crystallized. In more marginal terrain and particularly in upland areas Anglican practice tended to be weaker. The reasons for this were various. In some of the uplands there had been a great growth of population and settlement since the medieval period. The difficult terrain was an inevitable handicap to any institution seeking to control the local communities, and there was also the problem of settlement patterns. Dispersed settlement (scattered farmsteads) or multi-nucleated settlement (a number of distinct townships in a single parish) predominated in much of the North and West instead of the nucleated-village parish that was common in southern England and which served the Church's purposes much better.[12] Manorialism was also weaker in many parts of the outlying provinces. Communities were less well controlled by landowners than in southern England, an important factor once the Church found itself heavily dependent on squirearchic influence.

There were also long-standing deficiencies of the ecclesiastical structure. One was the diocesan pattern. Most of the dioceses outside southern England had been unwieldy in size and shape and, given the nature of terrain and communications, difficult to manage. Large parts of dioceses like York, Chester, Lincoln and Exeter had been beyond effective episcopal control.[13] The fringes of units of ecclesiastical organization had always presented problems and in the outlying provinces those fringes were very large indeed. Many of the outlying sees had also been among the poorest in income and they had suffered over the centuries from episcopal non-residence and frequent translations. There were similar problems at the parochial level. Parishes were generally much larger in the outlying dioceses. In the southern counties they averaged 2500 acres or less, but in the North-West and the Border counties that figure rose above 10,000 acres,[14] a size which, even with a sparse population, meant ineffective pastoral superintendence and a disincentive to the more distant parishioners to attend church. Attempts at various times to establish rural chapelries had never really been effective. Population growth had left larger proportions of the inhabitants of such parishes too isolated from churches and clergy for regular worship, even if performance of some of the rites de passage continued, and many large parishes had provided fertile ground for Dissent after 1660 and even more so for Methodism later. There were also financial problems. Most parishes in the peripheral dioceses had always been poor by southern standards and they seem to have suffered rather worse from tithe impropriations. These regional inequalities persisted despite later improvements in the value of clerical livings, and figures collected in 1831 showed the average values in the outlying dioceses (except for Durham which had benefited from mineral exploitation on Church land) to be well below those in southern England.[15] Financial stringency handicapped the running of parishes and encouraged low standards of clerical duty and provision in areas where the clergy were often thin on the ground anyway. It encouraged pluralism and, given the unattractiveness of much of the provincial periphery to educated and ambitious clergymen, the gravitation of clerical talent southwards. Though a former paucity of 'learned' clergymen outside southern England had been largely overcome, numbers of clergy of fairly humble origins and of a kind unfamiliar in the metropolitan region could still be found in the outer provinces.

All this had helped to regionalize religious practice well before the period we are considering. The Reformation Church had won firmest support in southern England while Catholic recusancy had survived best in parts of the far North and West, particularly in economically backward and remote areas beyond the influence of Protestant ideas and the arm of central government. Some of these pockets of Catholic support, particularly in the North, survived into the nineteenth century.[16] By then Protestant Dissent had also exploited some of these 'dark corners of the land'. As for Anglican practice itself, it seems unlikely that it reached levels in the outer dioceses as high as those in southern England even during the period of legal pressure before 1689. The circumstances of many parts of the English periphery in the first half of the nineteenth century suggest an age-old condition that had always frustrated ideals of conformity rather than a sudden and recent decline in Anglican practice. The account of the Eskdale parish of Danby left by its Victorian incumbent J. C. Atkinson illustrates conditions familiar in the rough, upland areas.[17] With 2300 inhabitants spread over 22,230 acres, Danby was six miles across and accessible only along rough tracks from Whitby. Severe moorland winters compounded the problem of having the church a mile away from the main centre of population, the patron was non-resident and the only laymen of substance were small farmers who shared the popular values. The parsonage was uninhabitable and the previous incumbent, of local origin and viewed by Atkinson as more peasant than gentleman, had shown no inclination to try to change the religious condition of the parish. There had once been Quakers in the neighbourhood and now Methodism was rife, but Atkinson encountered a strong local culture of folklore and superstition which he regarded as more pagan than Christian. He admitted that for many people Methodism had been the only alternative to irreligion. It is hard to believe that, Quakers and Methodists apart, Danby had ever been very different. A virtually unmanageable parish, it was perhaps an extreme case but it provides an insight into the difficulties the Church faced in considerable parts of the English periphery.

Dissent and Nonconformity

Like the unevenness of Anglican practice, much of the pattern of Victorian Dissent had originated long before the start of the nineteenth century. The Protestant Dissenters left outside the Church by the failure of comprehension after 1660 had been heavily concentrated in the more advanced parts of the country, notably in the large towns and the industrial and maritime districts. Dissent had also exploited the Church's weaknesses in country areas,[18] but the tide of rural Dissent seems to have receded in the eighteenth century leaving the denominations more urban in their basis than before. But the denominations of seventeenth-century origin – the Independents or Congregationalists, the Baptists, and, though less numerous, the Presbyterians (now mostly transmuted into Unitarians) and the Quakers – remained a force to be reckoned with and some of them were experiencing expansion again by 1800. In 1851 the old Dissent taken as a whole accounted for around a fifth of all attendances. Strongest of all in some of the older towns, it was also clearly regionalized in its distribution. The pattern differed from one denomination to another, but the sum total of the old Dissent was strongest in a belt running from East Anglia through the South Midlands into the inner West Country. In its stronghold of the eastern counties it returned an IA of around 25 and claimed about a third of all attendances.[19] Here Methodism had also won a significant following, though well short of its achievements further north and west.[20] Most of this region possessed a strong Anglican parochial structure (the old Dissent had originated as much in Church policy as in the establishment's territorial weakness) and the Anglican IA was over 40 in nearly all the counties in question, though inevitably the PS was rather less impressive. Aggregate attendances were higher than anywhere else outside Wales, and Bedfordshire returned the highest aggregate IA for any registration county. In the Bristol hinterland and the textile districts of the West Country the old Dissent also commanded attendances well above its national average, and elsewhere, in the Kentish Weald and parts of South Yorkshire for example, pockets of local strength had survived from the seventeenth century.

If eastern England south of the Wash provided the most spectacular support for the old denominations, there were parts of the periphery where they had waxed strong too. In the North-East, particularly in Northumberland, Scottish influence and immigration had created substantial support for Presbyterianism. In Wales the new evangelical versions of the old denominations had flourished mightily in the upsurge of popular religion since the mid-eighteenth century and, with the aid of Methodism which was particularly strong in North Wales, had turned the principality into the most Nonconformist region of all. Only in the North-East were Anglican attendances low enough to compare with those in Wales. The Church was structurally weak in Wales and negligent in its standards of clerical duty and provision. Patterns of scattered settlement in the large upland areas had posed problems and the rapid industrial growth in parts of South Wales had only compounded the existing difficulties. Most important of all perhaps were the problems associated with the Welsh language and with Welsh identity and feeling which left the Church identified with Englishness and Anglicization. By 1851 the Church's position was dangerously exposed in Wales. Here it was unquestionably a minority faith and was even more dependent on the support of the landed and professional classes than in England itself.

Thus by 1851 there had been a transformation of the pattern of religious practice and a growth of Nonconformity well beyond the confines of the old Dissent. Most remarkable of all had been the rapid growth of Methodism, especially in large areas of the North and West. The new Nonconformity was not homogeneous. Nor can it be attributed to a single cause, but the importance of demographic and economic factors was obvious. Population growth, always a threat to established religion, had been rapid by historical standards, the population of England and Wales doubling between 1801 and 1851. Levels of Anglican practice were threatened in the growing towns and in many rural areas where demographic pressure changed patterns of settlement. Certain kinds of Nonconformity had the appetite and flexibility to exploit these opportunities, and Methodism in particular, with its circuit system, itinerancy and lay preachers, was equipped to cope with a growing population and with rural conditions. Areas of weak Anglican provision were most vulnerable to Nonconformist expansion, and as it happened many of these areas had particularly high rates of population growth. Demographic pressure was often greatest where the establishment was least capable of a response. One measure of what this entailed was the availability of church room. In 1851 sittings in Anglican places of worship could hold 58.1% of the population in Rutland and 51.8% in Dorset, but only 21.6% in the West Riding, 19.3% in Lancashire and 18.0% in Durham.[21] There was a correlation, though not an exact one, between recent population growth and Anglican performance. The faster the demographic increase, the lower Anglican attendances tended to be.

The counties with the highest rates of population growth all contained concentrations of industrial development. Growing industries attracted labour, migration weakened old habits of religious practice (if any), industrial communities were usually outside the control of the Anglican squirearchy and new settlements lacked Anglican churches, clergy and schools. Rural or semi-rural industrial expansion, considerable over the decades before 1851, posed just as many problems as urban industrialization did. Much of the new industry was concentrated in parts of the country like the North Midlands, the Pennines, the North-East, South Wales and Cornwall where the Church was weak in organization and poorly equipped to respond. Much of the industrialization along the Pennines, for example, was in extremely large parishes with settlement patterns that made it difficult for the Church to resist Methodist advance. In Cornwall too the growth of the extractive industries added to older problems that included the county's isolation, patterns of settlement and Celtic cultural survival. Other parts of the country experienced little industrialization or even a decline of older industrial employment. This regionalization of industrial change helped to shape that of religious performance.

Much the same can be said of urbanization. Large towns had always been difficult for the Church to control and levels of religious conformity inevitably suffered from the rapid urban expansion of the early nineteenth century. The larger the town, the faster its growth rate and the more industrial its character, the lower its level of religious practice – and particularly Anglican practice – was likely to be. Of the thirty-seven towns outside London that gained more than 20,000 inhabitants between 1801 and 1851, thirty were north of that imaginary line from the Severn to the Wash. The greatest urban growth was thus in parts of the country where the Church was weak in organization, resources and influence. Urbanization did not create the regional differentiation of religious practice but it accentuated it.

These factors – population growth, industrialization and urbanization – did not always operate in conjunction. In Cornwall, Nottinghamshire and Derbyshire, for example, rapid population increase and industrial expansion were accompanied by relatively little urban concentration. In Lancashire and the West Riding, on the other hand, the growth of towns was a major feature. In Lincolnshire, where there was little industrialization and few towns of considerable size, an increase of population more dramatic than in most predominantly agricultural counties combined with rapid agricultural change to weaken the Church and to fuel Methodist growth. In all these counties the Church fared poorly in 1851. Major economic change of almost any kind was likely to work against the established Church. Only in a largely static society could a Church slow to adapt and highly dependent on habit, convention and traditional forms of influence hope to survive unscathed, and it was in the parts of the country that experienced little and slow change (like Dorset and Suffolk, the counties with the highest Anglican IAs) that religious conformity held up best.

The broad regional pattern has to be qualified by an allowance for the internal diversity of the regions and their constituent counties. There was almost as much variation and diversity among the registration districts of a large county like Devon as among the counties of England, and within the districts there often existed similar differences among the communities. The printed Census figures, which deal with no areas smaller than registration districts, fail to do justice to this local diversity. Historians have come to see that different types of local communities tended to produce corresponding types of religious culture and performance. The broad regional characteristics that we have noted depended to a considerable extent on the prevalence within the regions of certain kinds of communities rather than others. We must now look more closely at this local differentiation.

The Countryside

Many people imagine the rural parish of the nineteenth century as a single integrated village dominated physically by the big house, the parsonage and the church (perhaps with its Church school) and socially by the squire and parson. Such parishes certainly existed but they were far from universal. Had they been, religious conformity would have been much stronger in many rural districts than it was in practice. There were certain preconditions for the Church's dominance and they were not to be found in all rural communities.

Settlement

One factor was the settlement pattern. The parish worked best given a single nucleated village with its inhabitants close to the church and easily supervised by the incumbent. Multi-nucleated or dispersed settlement put much of the population distant from churches and clergymen and so was less conducive to high levels of Anglican practice and gave more scope to Nonconformity. The larger the parish, the less likely it was to have a single, concentrated settlement. We have seen that small single-village parishes were commonest in southern England and large parishes with the other forms of settlement in the North and West, but examples of the various types could be found in most counties. The disjunction between settlement and parochial structure had increased over the centuries as local economies and population changed while the medieval parochial structure remained unaltered, and increasing numbers of people found themselves remote from churches and clergy. Sometimes the church township had ceased to be the main settlement, as in Atkinson's Danby. Peripheral settlements tended to be outside the control of landowners and they sometimes had a reputation for turbulence as well as for what the clergy saw as immorality and heathenism. Others had a tradition of religious independence. In some of the large West Riding parishes Methodism made its earliest progress in out-townships that could trace their religious heterodoxy back to Lollard times. Good examples of the centre/periphery dichotomy occurred even in regions of Anglican dominance. Take the parishes of Cropredy and

Swalcliffe in North Oxfordshire. Served by different types of parsons in the early nineteenth century (the personal factor seems to have been unimportant), the two church villages remained solid for the Church while various sorts of Methodism took root in the outlying chapelries and settlements, though Cropredy's hamlet of Claydon, isolated and without resident landowners, was distinguished by crime, not by Nonconformity. Only in mid-century did a programme of church-building directed by an unusually determined bishop bring Anglican provision to these outlying settlements.[22]

Settlement and its relationship with parochial structure were a matter of terrain, of economics and of historical evolution. What had been prosperous villages in the medieval period usually retained an effective parochial structure and were conducive to dominant Anglican practice. More marginal lands settled at a later date usually had weaker parochial organization. Many of these areas were uplands, but not all of them. In Lindsey the former marshlands filled that role while the Wolds, settled much earlier, remained an area of strong Churchmanship.[23] Forests too could shape the local religious geography even after their disafforestation and enclosure, like Wychwood in North Oxfordshire, a good example of the woodland areas that gave the Church trouble and sometimes figured prominently in the history of Nonconformity. In 1809 Arthur Young had wanted its 7000 acres enclosed for social and moral rather than agricultural reasons. The forest harboured a disorderly community that busied the sessions and demoralized the neighbourhood. From 1830, as Church and aristocracy moved to impose order on the countryside, local landowners strove to suppress Wychwood Fair and the forest, originally extra-parochial, was being assigned to neighbouring parishes. The Wychwood Disafforesting Act of 1853 brought enclosure at last and separate parochial status. But the area continued to resist conformity and to trouble clerical and lay authorities. Its clergy complained of 'the Dissent of the majority' and as a centre of agricultural trade unionism in the 1870s it produced the Chipping Norton case, a *cause célèbre* that damaged relations between the Church and organized labour and brought the position of clerical magistrates into question.[24] Most counties, even those distinguished by good Anglican performance, contained problem enclaves like Wychwood.

Landownership

Another important factor was landownership. Parishes where the land was owned by one person or by very few large proprietors tended to remain safe for the Church. Parishes with widely distributed ownership were less amenable to Anglican influence and often provided good soil for Dissent. 'Landed property very much divided. Dissent much among them' was a familiar complaint in visitation returns.[25] The proprietary dominance of the aristocracy and gentry was a main prop of religious conformity. Landlords might refuse land for Nonconformist chapels (though preventing cottage meetings was harder), exclude Dissenters from their tenantry and generally use their position to discourage any challenge to the Church. Dissent found it hard to win a foothold where manorial control was strong and the extreme type of the estate village was the most inhospitable territory of all. Ensuring whole-hearted Churchmanship among tenants, dependants and villagers was more of a problem and not all landlords tried to compel regular church-going, but by the early Victorian period, as spiritual revival in the Church coincided with a defensive reaction among the aristocracy, landowners were exerting more effort than before on the Church's behalf, particularly in building and restoring churches and in promoting schools. But narrowly concentrated ownership was far from universal and its incidence varied from county to county and from parish to parish. Most parts of England had significant numbers of open or freeholder parishes. Widely-shared ownership meant an absence or weakness of pressure from above, meant more people to provide or sell sites for Nonconformist chapels, meant a spirit of social and political independence which, if it sought more than the occasional rites of the parish church, might find something more congenial than a church run by parsons, bishops and patrons, and meant more of those middling people whom the clergy often found to be opponents rather than collaborators. Open parishes usually had higher rates of population growth than closer parishes and were more likely to sustain industrial employment, and the base these parishes provided for religious independence had been greatly expanded by 1851. But this independence could also take the form of religious indifference and there were open villages, particularly in regions where Dissent was weak, with poor Anglican performance and no Nonconformity.

All this was a tendency, not an absolute rule. Some open parishes remained without Dissent. Some landlord parishes had a Nonconformist presence and this was more likely when the owner was non-resident, the big house was distant or the parish was difficult to control because of the settlement pattern or the occupational structure. There were also landlords, particularly those who were not patrons of livings, who were fairly indifferent to the nature of local religious practice and who, for whatever reasons, declined to exert much influence on the Church's behalf. Some just preferred to work with the grain of local society and to maintain relations with whatever denominations they found. In certain localities early Methodism had received encouragement from landed families and sometimes tolerance continued even after Methodism had separated from the Church. Though there were hardly any Nonconformists among large proprietors, there were occasional Roman Catholics and, in a few counties, significant numbers of them. Where they existed their behaviour could be the despair of incumbents.[26] In all these ways landowners could influence local patterns of religious performance.

Occupations

Occupational structures also mattered. In general the Church did best in predominantly agricultural districts, though even there Nonconformist meetings had been increasing since the start of the century, particularly in certain parts of the country, and even agricultural parishes without a Dissenting presence could return low Anglican attendances. Developments in the farming economy had probably damaged the Church by widening class divisions and weakening communal solidarity. Even before 1851 the appeal of Primitive Methodism to labourers in some rural areas was making it something of a class denomination. Any reshaping of religious attitudes for these or other reasons was bound to add to the differentiation of the local communities simply because people were freer to follow their own inclinations in some places than in others. Even without Dissent there were variations in levels of Anglican performance, some of them connected with forms of agricultural practice. Pastoralism, because of its work routines and the types of terrain and settlement often associated with it, seems to have been less conducive than arable cultivation to churchgoing.[27]

Within the localities some occupational groups were more likely to support the Church than others. Farmers, a key element, are rather difficult to categorize in this respect. Their religious allegiances were affected by the regional and local factors we have already noted, and with tenant farmers much probably depended on the landlords. Small farmers were perhaps more given to Nonconformity than were larger farmers with aspirations to gentility, and freeholder farmers more so than tenants. The predominance of small and often poor farms in Wales and parts of provincial England contributed to the local difficulties experienced by the Church. In all agricultural communities the Church found it difficult to attract certain types of workers – craftsmen and farm servants for example – and young unmarried men tended to be beyond religious influence. Village craftsmen often provided support for Nonconformity and parishes with substantial numbers

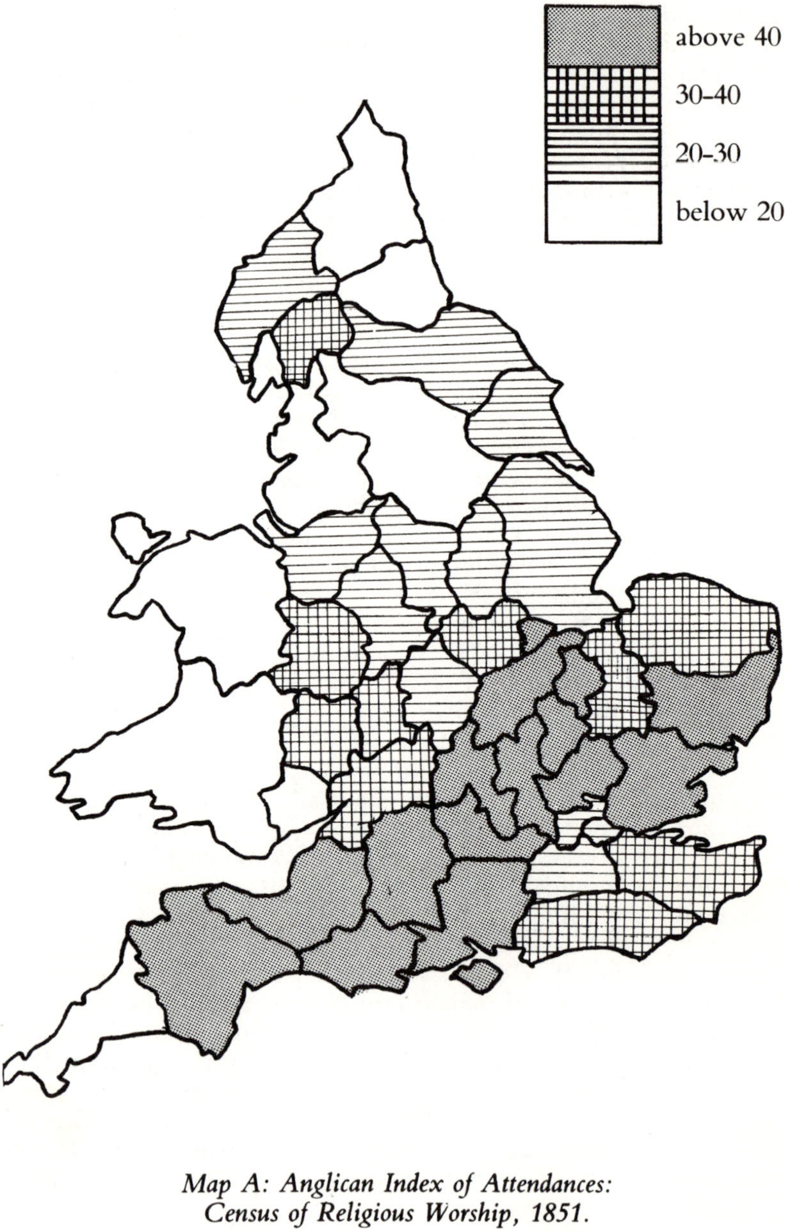

Map A: Anglican Index of Attendances: Census of Religious Worship, 1851.

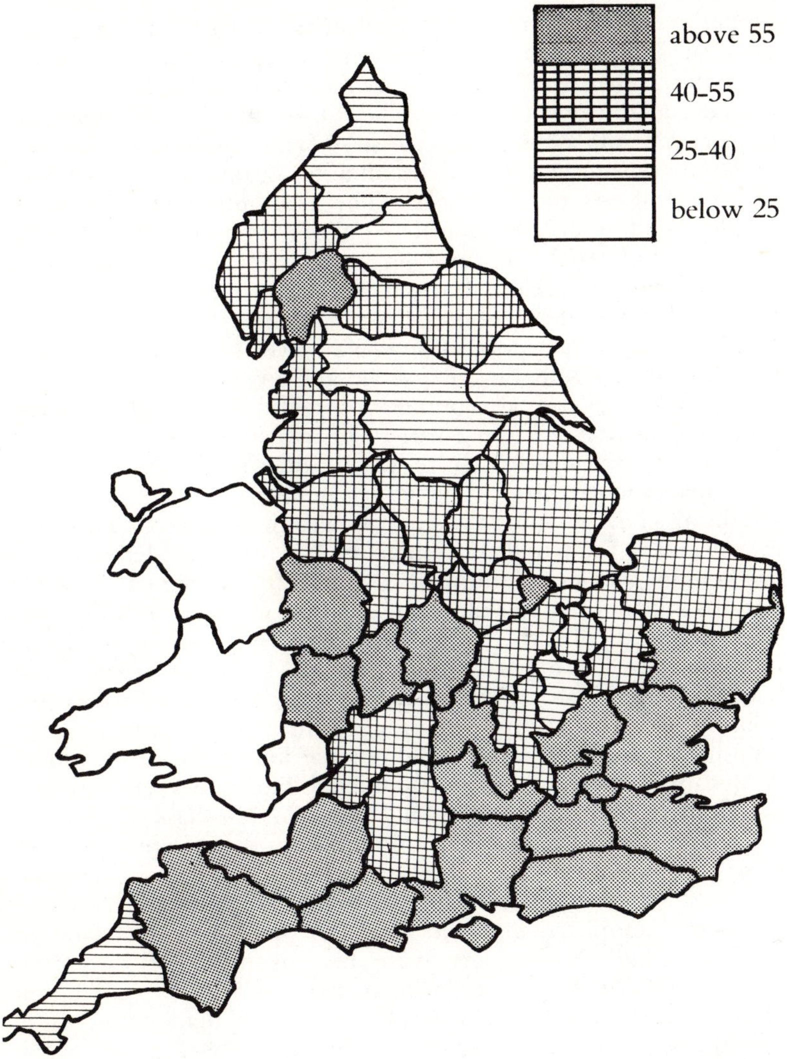

Map B: Anglican Percentage Share of Attendances: Census of Religious Worship, 1851

NOTE: Both maps are based on the figures for registration counties given in Table C. Though the London registration division is shown, the figures on which the shading of the surrounding counties is based include the metropolitan parts of those counties.

of such workers were rarely easy ones for the Church. Nonetheless, predominantly agricultural districts, though they were subject to regional and local factors, were usually kinder to the Church than were mixed or non-agricultural localities.

George Eliot once contrasted the 'rustic stupidity' and religious conformity of a Midland parish's farm labourers with the 'obstreperous animalism' of the miners and the 'acrid Radicalism and Dissent' of the weavers.[28] The assumption that industrial employment worked against Anglican interests was largely justified. Industrial workers were usually beyond the forms of social control that buttressed conformity, and rapid industrialization of the kind that created new settlements and drew in a large immigrant population was particularly damaging. Rural industrial employment had expanded in many areas in the first half of the century and all counties contained industrial or semi-industrial districts. A great variety of industrial occupations, not just miners and weavers, were leaving their mark on the map of religious practice. In putting larger numbers of people beyond Anglican control industrialism had also helped Nonconformist expansion, as the woollen manufacture had done for Methodism in the Pennine parishes of the West Riding and as mining had done for various kinds of popular Nonconformity in many parts of Durham and Cornwall. In their 'frontier town' phase new industrial communities were often distinguished by a disorderly and hedonistic popular culture that allowed little place to formal religion. Reaction against this was more likely to find expression in a Nonconformity that embodied popular independence than in an Anglicanism dominated by traditional hierarchies and by the values of the educated and usually upper middle-class clergy.

Quite apart from industrial concentrations there were districts in nearly all counties with substantial numbers of non-agricultural workers. Coastal and riverside districts, for example, had their distinctive employments and ways of life. Sailors, boatmen, fishermen and wildfowlers were free of many of the social disciplines that helped to sustain the Church in agricultural communities. Coastal districts also came into contact with outside influences, including foreign ones, and this was a factor in the multiplicity of faiths that existed in the small ports of Devon, for example.[29] Indeed it helped to explain the traditional heterodoxy of the long coastline of the South-West. The established Church had not always provided well for such localities. Some of the more barren and inhospitable coastal districts had suffered not only from a weak parochial system but also from the reluctance of the clergy to serve. East Mersea in Essex which Sabine Baring-Gould served in the 1870s and Morwenstow, the Cornish parish of his biographical subject R. S. Hawker, were two places of this kind.[30]

Even in agricultural areas there were small towns, market villages and other sizeable communities which, though small by city standards, played a key role in the local economy and were not easily dominated by squires and parsons. Some of them sustained good Anglican performance, but their occupational diversity and the existence of numbers of tradesmen, craftsmen and small employers gave scope for Nonconformity and other forms of resistance to the Church and its associated hierarchies. The case of Embleton in Northumberland, admittedly a problem county for the Church, illustrates these difficulties. A large parish with several townships, it contained Presbyterians of Scottish origin as well as large numbers of quarrymen and some fishing communities on the coast. The central township was 'a sort of metropolis' to a considerable area, lacked a resident squire and was dominated by numerous tradesmen and small employers, some of them owning the pubs and all 'on much the same level of cultivation as those they employed'. This was a recipe for a troublesome parish. Mandell Creighton, one of Embleton's Victorian incumbents, found it to be a turbulent and 'immoral' township in which the main influences worked against the Church and what it sought to achieve.[31] At best the employers and other middling men of such places were a counterweight to the influence of squires and parsons. At worst they might be Nonconformists proselytizing for their own denominations, like the farmer-clothiers who helped to spread Methodism in the West Riding. In such cases the Church had to work against the grain of local economic relationships. At Chipping Norton, where the Dissent associated with the old woollen industry remained vigorous, there were clerical complaints of 'a positive premium on Dissent in the fact of the chief employers of the people being Dissenters and almost openly preferring those of their own denomination'.[32]

The independence of certain communities and occupational groups could take political as well as religious forms. In the social conflicts of the century's first half the Anglican clergy usually identified themselves with established authority. Some of them were involved as magistrates in the repression of popular disturbance. If the Church's politics were scarcely the main reason for its local problems, the increase of social tension certainly found the Church poorly equipped to capture popular sympathy. This was a general problem in a society dividing more on class lines but a particular difficulty in the localities that suffered most from the strains of economic change, like parts of the industrial North and Midlands affected by Luddism and Chartism and the districts in southern England where the discontents of agricultural labourers boiled over in 1830. It can, however, be difficult to estimate the contribution of political tension to the Church's position in particular localities and especially to relate earlier events to the patterns of worship revealed by the 1851 Census. What one can say is that localities with major problems of political control were likely to produce weak Anglican practice anyway.

Religious conformity was anyway influenced by more than the immediate local factors. Outside influences could matter too. Industrial or urban developments could affect quite large rural areas around them. This could happen in a variety of ways: for example, by changing marketing and communications patterns, by intensifying labour-migration, by raising wage levels (one factor in popular independence)[33] and by creating centres from which Nonconformity could be diffused. In 1821, for example, Plymouth, Devonport and Saltash were sources of itinerant preachers for large areas of West Devon and East Cornwall.[34] Towns which served as putting-out centres for domestic industry could have a marked influence on the rural districts around them and there were many towns like this in the North and the Midlands in the first half of the century. The Church's diminishing hold on parts of rural Nottinghamshire and Leicestershire had been attributed to the dependence of local industrial workers on urban employers.[35] Local religious practice, therefore, often has to be seen in a wider context than the immediate locality, though there were also many rural parishes pretty well insulated by their location and economic character from serious external influence.

Ecclesiastical provision

The nature of Anglican provision was another factor in local religious performance. There was some relationship between parish size and levels of church-going and it was unusual to find high Anglican attendance in parishes of large area or population. Small parishes were easier to manage and usually produced better attendance figures. As we noticed with multi-township parishes, the location of churches was also important. The church might even be isolated from any major settlement, a serious deterrent to regular worship by the population, especially in winter. It is less clear how much the performance and character of individual incumbents affected religious practice. The non-residence of incumbents, which seems to have increased in the late eighteenth century and against which effective moves began only in the 1830s, has often been seen as a major cause of Anglican weakness. The lack of resident incumbents, particularly when continued over several generations as happened in some parishes, hardly encouraged religious conformity, and Methodist evangelists often concentrated on parishes without pastoral care. The relationship between non-residence and the presence of Dissent is, however, unclear.[36] The technical non-residence of incumbents was also not the same as a complete lack of provision for services and the latter was unusual. Clerical provision anyway tended to be worst in just those places where other factors were working against religious conformity. What mattered was the sum total of the influences working in a locality for and against Anglican practice. Individual incumbents could certainly affect attendances and other aspects of parochial life, but more permanent features of the localities seem to have done more to shape their religious performance.

Perhaps the same can be said of disputes over tithe and enclosure in the first half of the century. Tithes were a major irritant in the years of agricultural depression after 1815, and many parishes suffered disputes before tithe-commutation came under the act of 1836.[37] The enclosure movement benefited many incumbents and helped to cement their alliance with the landowning elites. How much it damaged their relations with other classes is more problematical. Though tithe and enclosure probably increased anti-clerical feeling, it is usually difficult to relate their impact to levels of Anglican performance in particular localities.

Several points stand out from this discussion. One is the great diversity of rural communities and of the influences that shaped them. This makes tidy generalization difficult. But different types of communities tended to produce corresponding forms of religious condition, ranging from the estate villages of zealously Anglican proprietors to freeholder parishes without resident squires and with a large industrial workforce. What shaped the religious culture of a locality was more the irreducible facts of geography, economics and social structure than those features one sees as specifically 'religious'. Though many elements in the local pattern had originated earlier, over the century leading to the Census of 1851 the Church and the religious conformity which it sought had fared best in conditions of two kinds. One was the 'steady state' community that changed little and slowly. The other was where influence from above protected and encouraged Anglican practice. These conditions were not mutually exclusive. Rapid demographic and economic change, however, tended to undermine social disciplines and to break patterns of custom in ways that worked against the Church and might help Nonconformity. The highly variegated local pattern of religious performance in 1851 showed not just the diversity of rural communities but also the varied nature and pace of the changes occurring in rural society and the unevenness of traditional kinds of social authority.

The Towns

We tend to regard the urban and the rural as homogeneous and antithetical categories, but the evidence of religious practice in nineteenth-century England suggests otherwise. Both the urban and the rural sectors of society were diverse enough to make simple generalizations hazardous and both of them provided examples of a great variety of religious conditions. Towns and rural communities sometimes had more in common with each other than they did with other places on their own side of the urban/rural divide. That divide was not always a clear one anyway, for there existed a great many small towns that could hardly be categorized as either simply urban or simply rural. Even with communities more easily categorized there was often considerable interaction between urban and rural sectors within the same region, so that town and countryside appeared as variants of the same regional pattern of religious performance rather than as opposites.

Size and Growth Rates

There were, however, clear differences between the large towns taken as a whole and smaller categories of communities. The aggregate of religious practice ran at much lower levels in the former than in the rest of English society. In London and the 65 'large towns' identified by the Census Report aggregate attendances for all denominations averaged about two-thirds of those for the rest of England and Wales. It was much the same picture for the Church of England. The Anglican IA was 20.3 against 31.4 for the rest of the country. The large towns were also notably pluralistic. In no town of any size and importance did the Church monopolize religious provision and practice as it did in many rural parishes. Even in towns with good Anglican attendances there were rival denominations present in numbers unusual in rural registration districts. Among the 65 large towns and eight metropolitan boroughs only eight recorded fewer than nine non-Anglican denominations and in seventeen cases fifteen or more sects were represented.[38] The range of denominations was greatest in the large cities but even smaller towns offered their inhabitants a considerable degree of consumer choice. The freedom to worship as one liked also implied the freedom not to worship at all.

If the large towns taken as a whole fell far short of Anglican ideals, individual towns spanned a wide range of religious performance. The aggregate IA of the 1851 Census ranged from Colchester's

Table A	Total	Anglican		Methodist		Indept.		Baptist		R. Cath.	
	IA	IA	PS	IA	PS	IA	PS	IA	PS	IA	PS
London & 65 towns	44.0	20.3	46.2	8.2	18.6	5.4	12.2	3.7	8.3	3.8	8.5
Rest of Eng. & Wales	65.6	31.4	47.9	18.5	28.2	7.3	11.2	5.8	8.2	1.1	1.7
Table B											
London (2.36m)	37.0	21.0	56.6	3.0	8.1	5.9	15.8	3.0	8.1	2.3	6.3
8 towns over 100,000	42.4	16.2	38.2	10.3	24.3	3.6	8.5	2.6	6.1	6.8	16.0
18 towns 50–100,000	49.4	18.7	37.9	11.7	23.6	6.3	12.8	5.4	10.9	3.1	6.2
29 towns 25–50,000	53.8	25.1	46.7	12.6	23.4	5.4	10.1	4.5	8.3	3.4	6.3
10 towns under 25,000	63.3	32.6	51.4	12.4	19.6	8.1	12.7	6.0	9.5	2.3	3.7

Attendances (uncorrected) in London and the 65 towns of the Report of the Census of Religious Worship, 1851

89.5 to Preston's 25.5, the Anglican IA from Exeter's 54.7 to Preston's 5.2 and the Anglican PS from Worcester's 70.3 to Merthyr Tydfil's 6.0. Despite the unease which many Anglicans felt about urbanization, not all the large towns presented a spectacle of disaster. The Church's IA exceeded the corrected national average in seventeen of the 65 Census towns and its PS did so in twenty. But they included only two towns with more than 50,000 inhabitants, a fact which underlined the tendency for Anglican performance to vary inversely with population size. Table B illustrates the point. London, easily the largest city, was an exception to the pattern, but otherwise Anglican attendance was depressed in the categories of large towns and improved significantly only among those with fewer than 50,000 inhabitants. The Church did notably well in the towns with under 25,000 inhabitants, its IA and PS exceeding those for the whole of the country outside the Census towns. Admittedly nearly all the towns in the last category were located in southern England, but even in most of the other regions Church attendances seem to have held up well in many of the towns too small for inclusion in the Census list. The traditional kind of small town had advantages which were not always to be found in newer or larger towns or even in many rural communities – like moderate rates of population and spatial growth, an adequate provision of churches, clergy and schools, the concentration of population near to the churches, and relatively large numbers of professional and educated people.

If size was a factor, so was growth rate. Most of the Census towns had grown rapidly over recent decades. The total population of the cities with over 100,000 inhabitants in 1851 had quadrupled in fifty years while the national population had doubled, but growth rates varied from town to town and the higher the rate, the lower Anglican attendances tended to be. Bristol recorded the slowest growth and the best Anglican attendances among the cities with over 100,000 inhabitants, while Bradford had the fastest growth and the worst Anglican IA. Bath and Preston provided a similar contrast in a different size-category. This was a tendency, not an exact causal relationship. When there were countervailing factors a town could combine, as Brighton did, strong Anglican performance with a high rate of growth. Like population size, the growth rate correlated with Anglican performance better for categories of towns than for individual communities.

The aggregate of all forms of religious practice suffered rather less from rapid urban growth than Anglican performance did. Some of the void left by the Church was filled by the voluntary denominations, and Protestant Nonconformity's share of attendances held up rather better than the Church's in the largest towns. By its nature the establishment was slower than its rivals to adapt to urban growth. Though the Million Act of 1818 had created a legal mechanism for building churches and dividing parishes, this movement for church extension in the towns entered top gear only in the 1830s, so that the provision of additional Anglican accommodation ran ahead of population growth for the first time in the decade 1841-51.[39] But church accommodation remained very unevenly distributed. While nine Census towns had fewer than 2000 inhabitants to every Anglican place of worship in 1851, eight towns, all of industrial or commercial character, had over 8000 inhabitants to every church. The extreme cases were Colchester with 1215:1 and Wigan with 10,647:1. Church provision was not the only influence on attendances, but it was one factor. Even people who queried the efficacy of simply building churches and dividing parishes had to reckon with the legacy of the Church's failure to cater for considerable sections of the urban population for a generation or more. As well as catering for further urban growth the Church needed to break ingrained habits of non-attendance at Anglican worship among much of the population and it was the largest and fastest-growing towns that tended to display the largest aggregations of the neglect of religious practice that contemporaries labelled 'spiritual destitution'. But in older, smaller and slower-growing towns like Colchester, Exeter and Worcester the parochial organization had never been overwhelmed, immigration had been absorbed more gradually and established religious practice had come under much less pressure.

Ethnic minorities

Another factor was the nature and pattern of immigration. England was a net importer of people from the rest of the United Kingdom, with its larger towns absorbing most of the immigrants, and many of them had acquired a considerable ethnic diversity. In the towns of the Border counties generations of Scottish immigrants had provided recruits for Presbyterianism. But the city with the greatest ethnic diversity was Liverpool. In 1851 28.6% of its adult inhabitants had been born in Ireland, 8% in Wales and 5.1% in Scotland, and the denominations most closely identified with those counties (the Catholics, Calvinist Methodists and Presbyterians) accounted between them for an IA of 18.0 and a PS of 39.7.[40] Large ethnic minorities always dented the Church's attendance figures and the large cities in which religious conformity held up well were nearly all ones with relatively small non-English immigrant communities. In most cities the largest minority was Irish and the Census figures showed their impact on religious practice. The Roman Catholic IA and PS exceeded the national average in all the categories of Census towns, particularly the largest, though London was an exception. As well as being heavily urbanized, Catholic strength showed a regional incidence, with the North-West its centre. Lancashire, a county with significant native recusancy, also contained the largest urban concentrations of the Irish and its Catholic attendances were predominantly Irish by

1851.[41] But fast-growing towns everywhere attracted Irish labour, and even where a shortage of Catholic chapels meant that they were under-represented in terms of attendances the size and ethnic solidarity of the Irish community affected the Anglican IA and the pattern of local religious practice.

Regional Influences

There was also the regional factor. Most towns reflected in some way the predominant religious characteristics of their regions, even if the larger towns usually returned aggregate and Anglican IAs rather lower than those for the rest of the region. In regions of Anglican strength most towns returned high Anglican attendances for communities of their size, and the reverse was true in regions of Anglican weakness. It followed that the regional pattern of Anglican performance was pretty well reproduced by the large towns. Of the seventeen Census towns with Anglican IAs above the corrected national average only four were north of that imaginary line across the middle of England. Not one of the thirty towns with an Anglican IA of twenty or less was south of the line. The congruence between towns and their regions can be seen in the figures in Tables C and D (p.40-2) and very few examples will have to suffice here. Birmingham, though much the larger city, returned considerably better Anglican attendances than Sheffield, which was broadly similar in economic character and growth-rate, and so reflected the Church's stronger showing in the West Midlands than in the West Riding. Cathedral cities also showed a regional bias. Anglican attendances in Carlisle, York, Lincoln and Chester contrasted unfavourably with those for Exeter, Worcester and Oxford. The case of London, though less straightforward, supports the same argument. Its aggregate attendances were much what one might have expected from the largest city, but its Anglican IA was above the average for the large cities and the PS exceeded even the national average. The capital seems to have been reproducing in a modified form the dominant characteristics of its region, and indeed the strength of the old Dissent in Essex and East Anglia was matched by its showing in East London.

Thus the interdependence or interaction of the towns and their regions, an idea familiar enough in the sphere of economics, had a religious dimension too. We have already seen how towns might affect the religious life of the rural districts around them, but influence could operate in the other direction too. One form of it was migration from countryside to town. The volume of migration had grown since the mid-eighteenth century and most large towns had a considerable proportion of recent immigrants of fairly local – or at least regional – origin. A straight transfer of rural religious behaviour into the towns cannot be assumed, but sources of immigration seem to have had some influence on the urban religious scene. One factor in the contrasting pictures presented by Devon's two large towns was that Plymouth had drawn 13% of its adult population in 1851 from strongly Nonconformist Cornwall but Exeter only 2.4%.

There were, of course, limits and exceptions to the importance of the regional factor. No town's religious condition was ever a mirror image of its hinterland. The heavy urban concentrations of the Catholic Irish, for example, had little rural equivalent. The clear differences among the large towns of the West Riding showed that the regional factor was only one among many. Towns with economic functions distinct from those of the surrounding areas were quite likely to produce a significantly different performance. Resort and retirement towns were a case in point and they were often more strongly Anglican than might otherwise have been expected. It took more than the regional factor to give Bath and Brighton Anglican attendances so much higher than those of other towns of similar size and growth-rate.

Industrialism

The Census list included a number of towns of predominantly industrial character. With these towns, particularly the newer ones, it is difficult to distinguish the effects of industrialism itself from those of concomitants like rapid urban growth and large-scale immigration or, indeed, from those of long-standing regional factors in Anglican performance. To attribute everything solely or even mainly to industrialism would be to beg many questions. But Anglican practice was undeniably poor in nearly all the industrial towns in 1851. In some of them Nonconformity was strong, in others all religious practice was at a low ebb, but nowhere did Anglican attendances exceed the national average and in most cases they ran at about half that level or less. Something like this might have been expected, given the size, growth-rate and regional location of most of the towns concerned. Another factor was the age and sex structure of growing industrial communities with their above-average numbers of younger men, an element among whom religion was notoriously weak. (Towns with high Anglican attendances usually had high proportions of unmarried women, many of them being servants.) Industrial towns, like most others, were also short of the forms of social control which Anglican landowners operated in many rural parishes. Large capitalist enterprises, particularly those with company estates, admittedly gave some scope for paternalism and there were employers who provided churches for their workpeople. Examples of this were Copley and Akroydon in Halifax, where the Akroyd family built churches alongside the worker's houses, and Rhymney in South Wales where the iron company's early provision of a church provided the Church with some success in an otherwise difficult area.[42] But such provision was far from general and paternalism, even where it existed, could just as easily work against the Church. Industrial entrepreneurs as a class were less solidly Anglican and less committed to social duty than the landed aristocracy were. Sir Titus Salt's Saltaire with its sole Congregational chapel left no room for an Anglican presence. Of the leading Staffordshire potters Job Ridgway worked for the Methodists, while Josiah Wedgwood's Etruria remained without any place of worship for over forty years and until well after its founder's death.[43] The Church was inevitably disadvantaged in the communities dominated by men like these.

But in many industrial towns there was no dominant influence to shape religious practice. Probably the larger part of the industrial workforce was left without religious provision and persuasion by employers and superiors. Given the growing segregation of the classes and the lack of Anglican churches and pastoral care in many working-class districts, there developed working-class cultures that gave little place to formal religion, particularly the Anglican kind. Although Nonconformity won a lower-class following in certain towns, regular Anglican practice was uncommon in most poor neighbourhoods and the Church retained a central role only as a provider of schooling and of the rites de passage.[44] Even when there was little popular hostility towards the Church, the clergy were likely to encounter an overwhelming indifference towards regular Anglican worship and often towards denominational religion in general.

The popular standing of the Church had suffered during the long period of social tension and economic instability from the 1790s to the 1840s. In industrial towns rent by conflict the identification of the Church and its clergy with government and employers may have bound local elites closer to the establishment but it scarcely helped relations with the lower classes at a time when so much else was weakening Anglican influence. In certain towns the hostility of the politicized sections of the working population towards the Church found clear expression, though this was only one influence among many on religious performance. It was probably also past its peak even in 1851 and the Church seems to have improved its popular standing in most towns with the easing of social tension in the following years. Its efforts for church extension and popular schooling were contributing something to this process, but probably more important was the way mid-Victorian industry was generating middle-class wealth of which part went to benefit the Church. If entrepreneurs had rarely supported the Church actively, their heirs and other beneficiaries of the mature industrial economy were doing so on a considerable scale. In 1878 the *Quarterly Review* listed many benefactors in the towns of industrial Yorkshire and wrote of 'the love for the Church of England which so largely prevails in the West Riding', and church extension in the new diocese of Manchester also found numerous subscribers, benefactors and patrons among the business and professional classes.[45] In any industrial town the size, nature and social development of the local elites had a considerable bearing on Anglican fortunes.

There was also to be the native reaction to Irish immigration. Lancashire, the county with the largest concentrations of the Irish, produced the strongest manifestations of 'popular Protestantism' among the working classes as well as their social betters. It was a mood which Evangelical Anglicanism was well fitted to exploit. (Here, as elsewhere, Tractarian or Ritualist Anglicanism won rather less popular sympathy.) Apart from its political importance, 'Protestantism' contributed to the success of Church Sunday schools in certain industrial towns, not all of them in Lancashire, in attracting large numbers of children and even young adults from the working classes. This was compensation for the damage that Irish immigration had done to the Church, but the dissipation of old political hostilities and the Church's new sense of confidence seem not to have been matched by a substantial improvement in working-class churchgoing. Indeed an account of industrial Lancashire was to complain that 'attendance at [Sunday] school is accounted a proof of Church membership, and is regarded as a valid excuse for absence from Church worship at the following services'.[46] New churches still met with greatest success in middle-class districts.

Generally depressing as the industrial towns were for the Church in 1851, they were not all alike. Some of the older industrial or semi-industrial towns like Leicester, Derby and Northampton returned reasonable Anglican figures. These places had experienced slower growth than the boom towns of the new industrialism and they included old incorporated boroughs where Anglican oligarchies drawn from the professions and the trading community had exercised political control over a long period. County towns in particular never lacked important Anglican establishments of their own. Leicester and Northampton lay in areas of fairly strong Churchmanship and we have already seen how regional influences helped to differentiate the religious performances of industrial towns. A great deal also depended on local occupational structure.

Older towns with their large numbers of small employers and skilled craftsmen possessed more religious potential than the towns dominated by large employers and a proletarianized workforce, though the former constituency was often better exploited by Nonconformity than by the Church.[47] In certain towns the Church was already benefiting from the increasing numbers of managers, supervisors, bookkeepers and other white-collar elements that provided more fertile ground for the denominations than the mass of industrial workers did. The Church had suffered from the lack of sizeable middle classes in new industrial communities, and the gradual thickening of those strata gave scope for some modest Anglican recovery in the decades after 1851 and especially for the exploitation of predominantly middle-class residential suburbs.

The Classes

In fact social structure was a key factor everywhere. Certain social groups were more inclined than others to Anglican adherence and practice, and in most towns the local elites were the prime Anglican constituency. This was less true of some parts of the country than of others (the old Dissent was well represented among the urban elites of the eastern counties, for example) and less true of some groups than of others (industrial employers were less likely than professional men to be Anglicans), but in every town the level of Anglican performance was affected by the size and nature of the 'genteel' community. Exeter's much more numerous body of professional men was one reason why its churchgoing exceeded Northampton's and Leicester's.[48] The overwhelmingly Anglican character of fashionable resorts like Bath and Cheltenham owed a great deal to unusually large bodies of the gentility and their dependents, and the larger the proportion of such people among a town's population the more luxuriant its Anglicanism was likely to be. Where they were scarce, Anglican observance suffered, not just from numerical deficiency but also from the lack of 'tone' in society, the weakness of elite influence on other social groups (shopkeepers for example) and the shortage of funds for Church activities. If one wants a class determinant of levels of Anglican practice, it probably lies here as much as anywhere. Much of the difference between the new industrial towns and the older urban communities in 1851 lay in the relative sizes of their educated and gentrified elites.

The Census Report argued that most of the absentees from public worship belonged to the urban working classes. In every large town considerable numbers of working people were obviously not regular church-goers. We have seen how Anglican provision had lagged behind the growth of working-class areas.

Even a cathedral city like Lincoln had poor districts unprovided with churches, schools and clergy. But the unevenness extended to much more than ecclesiastical provision,[49] and the latter's inadequacies were far from being the only explanation of working-class neglect of worship. Most large towns, whatever their overall character, were a patchwork of neighbourhoods of varying social composition and the incidence of Anglican practice usually reflected this differentiation. Most towns of the period were experiencing a growth in the functional specialization of areas and in the spatial separation of the classes for residence. Many contemporaries deplored this 'separation of classes' as a factor in inadequate religious observance, among other social ills. The suburban drift of the prosperous and propertied left many city-centre parishes with little but working-class inhabitants. These neighbourhoods and also newly-developed working-class districts were difficult for the Church to influence even when it got around to trying and the fewer middle-class people there were the harder it was. As Orwell was to put it later, the solidly working-class districts without 'petty gentry' were the ones most resistant to 'embourgeoisification'.[50] Here most people felt few pressures to religious conformity. Even in the more respectable working-class neighbourhoods there was a vast gulf between the values and practices of educated Anglicanism and those of the inhabitants, there was little lay assistance for the clergy, the problems of parochial finance were often crippling, and the level of 'respectability' associated with regular church-going was too difficult and too expensive for most working people. Whatever the numbers of children in Church day and Sunday schools, adult church attendances were nearly always well below those in the prosperous parts of the same town.

For all its difficulties in working-class districts the Church was not altogether a loser from class segregation and the development of class sub-cultures. Its success in fashionable neighbourhoods and in the expanding residential suburbs was just as significant. Here the provision and maintenance of new churches and the running of new parishes were comparatively easy, finance caused few problems and the pressures of social conformity worked in the Church's favour. The sense of propriety and respectability, aspirations to gentility (here the Church gained from its association with the aristocracy), the leisure-time available to middle-class women, the freeing of families for Sunday worship by the employment of servants, all assisted the profession and practice of conventional Anglicanism. The residential suburbs gave the Victorian Church a major growth-area and success story. Anglicanism usually enjoyed greater success in wealthy and solidly middle-class localities than in lower middle-class districts where there was less of the sense of social duty and the assertion of gentility that assisted the Church among the more fashionable. In lower middle-class neighbourhoods aggregate attendances at worship were usually lower and Nonconformity tended to take a larger share of them.[51]

The unevenness of Anglican practice in the towns is largely hidden by the printed Census figures. Only for London does it show in any detail. Attendances in the capital followed much the same pattern as church provision which was considerably more ample in the West End and suburban districts than in those waterfront and semi-industrial areas with predominantly working-class populations. (Hampstead, the best provided registration district, had an Anglican church to every 1998 inhabitants; Old Street, the worst-off, one to every 13,514.) St George's, Hanover Square, in the West End returned the best Anglican PS (86.8), but the highest Anglican (and, for that matter, aggregate) IAs were recorded by a number of suburban and predominantly residential districts. Hampstead's Anglican IA of 56.9 and PS of 82.2 made it something of a suburban idyll for the Church.[52] At the opposite end of the scale was an assortment of poor districts with notably low Anglican attendances. Shoreditch returned an Anglican IA of only 6.2.

In most of these districts the Church accounted for around a third of all attendances, well below its average for London, and in Old Street the PS fell to 15.9, though in Bethnal Green, a parish subject to intensive sub-division and church-building since the 1830s, the Church had half the aggregate attendances. The range of variation among the metropolitan districts was greater for Anglican attendances than for aggregate attendances, Nonconformity and Roman Catholicism making up some of the deficiency where the Church was weakest.

London was scarcely a typical town, but much the same relationship between the class character of localities (as expressed in rateable values and ratios of servant-keeping) and Anglican practice was common in the large towns throughout the Victorian period.[53] In urban society, even more than in the countryside, the Church had become something of a class church, at least in respect of regular worship. Local patterns were never absolutely fixed and they could be modified by the character and performance of individual ministers, by good preaching (though that often raised attendances by attracting worshippers from other churches) and by energetic pastoral work. The example of Bethnal Green suggests that efforts to improve Anglican provision could also reap some reward. In general, though, all these things were of temporary and marginal impact when set against the more permanent influences of economics and class.

Several main points emerge from this discussion. One is that urban society, like its rural counterpart, took many forms. Indeed the degree of social and economic differentiation among urban communities in mid-century was probably greater than ever before. Though no two towns were identical, there were certainly distinguishable types of towns and each tended to produce a corresponding type of religious condition. But there was considerable differentiation within individual towns as well as between them and probably the larger the town the greater its internal diversity was likely to be. A further point is that the towns need to be studied in their regional contexts, for the urban and rural religious conditions were better integrated than has often been assumed. It is clear that religious conformity had been maintained best where towns had experienced only gradual change and had suffered most where change had been greatest and swiftest. This was true of rural communities too, but the paternalistic control that sheltered the Church in many rural parishes was less common in the towns. There religious practice was more a matter of personal choice and much less often dictated or restricted from above. Partly because of this lack of social authority to impose the official faith across class boundaries, Anglican practice, particularly regular worship, had more of a class character in urban society than in the countryside. The class structures and sub-cultures that worked both to the detriment and to the benefit of the Church in 1851 went on doing so for the rest of the century, but even in mid-century the contrast between, say, middle-class residential suburbs and working-class industrial districts within the same town could be as sharp as any between towns of very different types.

Conclusion

The variation in levels of Anglican practice revealed by the Census of Religious Worship was a natural consequence of the nature and the geographical incidence of social and economic change over several centuries at least, though some of the sharpest contrasts were of relatively recent origin. 1851 was not the end of change. A further census of religious worship at the end of the century would have revealed a number of differences from the picture of 1851, even if the main outlines remained intact. By then the Salvation Army had arrived, the Baptists had enjoyed a notable mid-Victorian growth and Methodism had made advances in London and the South-East. Continued Irish immigration and the late-Victorian influx of East European Jews had swollen the ethnic groups outside Anglican influence.

On the whole, though, the Church's own fortunes seem to have been rather happier in the century's second half than in the first. The prospect which some had seen in the 1830s of an almost total collapse of Anglican allegiance and practice had receded. Church extension and an improvement in pastoral zeal and efficiency had helped to stabilize the Church's position and to produce a long-term improvement in national figures of communicants and confirmations, though it is not clear whether church-going increased similarly.[54] It seems likely, however, that most of the influences on Anglican practice after 1851 were beyond the Church's control and were similar to those that had operated before that date: demographic trends, migration and immigration, changes in residential patterns and class behaviour, the growth or decline of industries, changes in the character of employment and in labour relations in agriculture and industry. The Church 'revival' which some historians have detected in the century's second half probably owed more to one of these factors, the rapid growth of the suburbanized middle classes, than to anything else. The lack of a further official census of worship makes the changes in the social geography of religious practice hard to map. Though various local and private surveys were conducted, their results were not always full, reliable and easily compared with those of 1851 and even in sum total they fell far short of a national coverage. London received the fullest treatment and only for the capital is a satisfactory picture available. Trends in Anglican practice outside the cities are particularly hard to follow.

It seems, however, that some of the regional variations in Anglican practice were weakening by the end of the century. The local censuses of the 1880s confirmed the broad picture of 1851[55] but some of the contrasts were now slightly less extreme. The growth of Methodism in and around London and the modest signs of Anglican 'revival' even in Wales were two illustrations of this evening-up tendency. Regionalism, it seemed, was passing its peak. Figures for Anglican communicants and confirmations show regional differences persisting into the second half of the twentieth century[56] but the extent of variation has lessened since the last century and the greatest differences now lie between the great conurbations and the rest of England. It also seems that as the urban concentration of the population has grown, the class pattern of Anglican practice has intensified. That development was certainly foreshadowed in the 1851 figures.

Though there remain certain local and regional variations in religious practice, both Anglican and non-Anglican, the general decline in Christian observance has made the whole question less central to our understanding of society. But the great diversity of religious expression during the nineteenth century, when denominational vigour, both inside and outside the established Church, co-existed with a neglect of regular religious practice by growing numbers, was of more than narrowly religious significance. It was part of wider social and economic developments and can be fully understood only in that context. The study of religion in this period, possibly more than in any other, requires some sense of social geography, of region and of locality, and of the various forces operating upon people's behaviour in each. This is clearly true of practice in the Church of England, national institution though it was.

Census of Religious Worship: 1851
Table C. Attendances in the Registration Counties (excluding City of York)

	Total	C. of E.	Methodists	Independents	Baptists	Rom.Cath.
	IA	IA/PS	IA/PS	IA/PS	IA/PS	IA/PS
England & Wales (uncorrected)	58.1	27.6/47.4	14.9/25.7	6.6/11.4	5.1/8.7	2.0/3.5
England & Wales (corrected)	60.8	29.5/48.6	15.2/25.0	6.8/11.1	5.2/8.5	2.1/3.5
Bedfordshire	104.6	41.0/39.3	28.8/27.5	9.2/8.8	20.8/19.9	0.1/0.1
Berkshire	66.0	40.1/60.7	12.8/19.4	6.2/9.4	5.0/7.5	0.8/1.2
Buckinghamshire	87.3	44.3/50.7	17.7/20.2	8.1/9.3	16.1/18.4	0.4/0.4
Cambridgeshire	84.3	37.1/44.0	18.1/21.5	8.6/10.2	17.3/20.5	0.4/0.5
Cheshire	52.3	24.3/46.5	17.5/33.4	4.5/8.6	1.1/2.2	3.0/5.7
Cornwall	68.0	19.2/27.2	43.8/64.5	2.8/4.1	1.3/2.0	0.3/0.4
Cumberland	37.3	20.0/53.7	9.4/25.3	2.7/7.2	0.3/0.9	2.1/5.6
Derbyshire	58.8	23.7/40.8	23.9/40.9	4.3/7.3	4.3/7.3	1.3/2.2
Devon	70.5	40.1/56.9	13.2/18.7	7.6/10.8	5.3/7.5	0.3/0.9
Dorset	77.6	48.2/62.1	13.8/17.7	11.7/15.1	1.6/2.1	0.7/0.9
Durham	42.6	14.4/33.8	19.6/46.0	2.1/5.0	1.4/3.4	3.0/7.0
Essex	73.3	42.2/57.5	6.2/8.5	16.9/23.0	6.0/8.2	0.6/0.8
Gloucestershire	65.5	34.4/52.3	10.5/16.0	9.3/14.2	10.2/15.5	1.6/2.5
Hampshire	67.6	40.5/59.9	10.0/14.8	10.4/15.4	4.6/6.8	1.0/1.4
Herefordshire	49.0	32.3/65.9	8.0/16.3	2.3/4.7	4.0/8.2	0.5/1.0
Hertfordshire	74.7	42.4/56.8	9.4/12.5	10.6/14.3	10.8/14.5	0.4/0.6
Huntingdonshire	94.2	42.3/44.9	20.5/21.8	6.7/7.1	20.6/21.9	-/-
Kent	56.9	38.9/68.5	8.6/15.1	5.2/9.1	5.4/9.4	0.8/1.3
Lancashire	44.1	18.8/42.6	9.9/22.4	4.2/9.5	1.8/4.0	7.2/16.3
Leicestershire	72.0	35.5/49.3	15.6/21.8	6.1/8.4	11.7/16.2	1.7/2.3
Lincolnshire	63.4	27.4/43.3	29.5/46.5	2.3/3.7	3.2/5.1	0.6/0.9
Middlesex	37.2	21.4/60.5	3.0/8.0	6.1/16.3	2.6/6.9	2.1/5.7
Monmouthshire	73.3	16.4/22.4	21.5/29.3	11.2/15.3	20.4/27.9	2.4/3.2
Norfolk	65.3	34.2/52.3	20.5/31.3	3.4/5.2	5.4/8.2	0.5/0.7
Northamptonshire	89.6	45.0/50.3	19.0/21.2	10.2/11.4	13.1/14.7	0.4/0.4
Northumberland	42.0	15.6/37.2	10.7/25.2	1.7/4.0	1.1/2.7	2.7/6.3
Nottinghamshire	58.0	24.0/41.4	19.1/33.0	3.0/5.2	5.8/10.0	1.2/2.0
Oxfordshire	69.0	40.3/58.5	12.9/18.7	4.2/6.1	4.7/6.8	0.8/1.2
Rutland	68.4	42.5/62.1	10.7/15.6	4.4/6.4	10.2/14.9	-/-
Shropshire	59.5	35.4/59.7	16.0/27.0	4.7/7.9	1.9/3.1	1.0/1.6
Somerset	70.3	43.2/61.5	12.5/17.8	6.8/9.7	5.3/7.5	0.6/0.9
Staffordshire	48.8	22.5/46.1	18.1/37.0	3.2/6.6	1.9/3.9	2.6/5.3
Suffolk	82.2	46.7/56.8	8.8/10.8	13.2/16.1	12.4/15.1	0.2/0.2
Surrey	41.9	26.5/63.2	2.7/6.5	5.8/13.8	3.9/9.4	2.2/5.2
Sussex	56.4	38.4/68.1	5.7/10.6	5.5/9.7	4.3/7.6	0.4/0.7
Warwickshire	48.9	27.5/56.3	6.3/13.0	3.4/6.9	4.3/8.8	2.8/5.8
Westmorland	50.1	30.7/61.2	11.9/23.7	2.0/3.9	0.6/1.3	1.2/2.3
Wiltshire	85.7	44.7/52.2	16.0/18.7	10.3/12.1	12.6/14.7	0.6/0.7
Worcestershire	54.9	30.6/55.7	13.9/25.3	2.9/5.3	4.1/7.4	1.8/3.2
Yorkshire (East Riding)	58.8	21.8/37.0	27.8/47.3	4.8/8.1	1.2/2.1	1.6/2.8
Yorkshire (North Riding)	63.6	26.4/41.6	28.8/45.4	3.5/5.6	1.2/1.9	2.4/3.8
Yorkshire (West Riding)	52.9	18.1/34.2	22.3/42.3	5.8/10.9	3.4/6.5	1.5/2.9
North Wales	86.6	15.1/17.4	48.9/56.4	13.8/15.9	7.4/8.5	0.3/0.4
South Wales	83.4	15.6/18.3	23.9/28.7	23.7/28.5	17.7/21.3	0.6/0.7

Notes on Tables C and D are printed on page 42.

Table D. Attendances in London and the 65 large towns

	Population	Total IA	C. of E. IA/PS	Methodists IA/PS	Independents IA/PS	Baptists IA/PS	Rom.Cath. IA/PS
London	(2,362,236)	37.0	21.0/56.6	3.0/8.1	5.9/15.8	3.0/8.1	2.3/6.3
Ashton-Under-Lyme	(30,676)	45.8	18.4/40.2	10.5/23.0	9.3/20.2	1.4/3.0	3.1/6.8
Bath	(54,240)	79.1	48.7/61.6	11.1/14.0	4.9/6.2	3.6/4.6	2.6/3.2
Birmingham	(232,841)	36.1	17.0/47.1	5.2/14.5	3.3/9.1	4.2/11.6	2.2/6.1
Blackburn	(46,536)	37.7	16.7/44.4	6.2/16.5	5.2/13.8	1.4/3.8	4.1/10.8
Bolton	(61,171)	36.8	15.3/41.7	8.6/23.4	4.2/11.5	0.9/2.5	4.8/13.1
Bradford	(103,778)	42.7	9.8/22.9	16.9/39.6	5.6/13.1	4.9/11.8	3.9/9.1
Brighton	(69,673)	52.5	31.5/60.0	6.4/12.2	4.5/8.5	5.6/10.7	1.3/2.5
Bristol	(137,328)	56.7	25.2/44.9	9.8/17.3	9.0/15.8	4.8/8.4	3.4/5.9
Bury	(31,262)	44.1	17.3/39.3	10.4/23.5	6.1/13.9	2.5/6.0	3.7/8.3
Cambridge	(27,815)	67.8	40.1/59.9	6.9/10.1	2.3/3.3	15.0/22.2	2.3/3.4
Carlisle	(26,310)	35.0	11.5/32.8	9.8/28.0	3.2/9.1	0.3/1.0	6.4/18.4
Chatham	(28,424)	54.3	26.2/48.2	12.8/23.5	6.8/12.6	6.0/11.1	1.9/3.6
Cheltenham	(35,051)	66.2	40.8/61.7	8.1/12.3	5.4/8.1	8.1/12.3	3.2/4.8
Chester	(27,766)	57.4	31.0/54.0	14.0/24.3	6.2/10.8	0.8/1.3	2.4/4.2
Colchester	(19,443)	89.5	43.5/48.6	8.2/9.1	22.7/25.4	10.5/11.7	0.7/0.8
Coventry	(36,208)	40.2	18.2/45.3	2.2/5.4	7.9/19.6	4.2/10.4	6.1/15.1
Derby	(40,609)	59.0	23.6/40.0	14.8/25.1	5.6/9.4	7.8/13.2	5.6/9.6
Devonport	(50,159)	56.5	22.0/39.0	14.3/25.3	10.6/17.9	6.1/10.7	2.0/3.5
Dover	(22,244)	67.1	47.1/70.1	8.2/12.2	4.2/6.2	5.7/8.5	-/-
Dudley	(37,962)	55.3	13.9/25.1	26.4/47.7	3.5/6.2	4.9/8.9	3.5/6.3
Exeter	(32,818)	84.5	54.7/64.7	10.0/11.8	3.6/4.3	7.0/8.3	0.8/0.9
Gateshead	(25,568)	32.9	13.2/40.0	15.4/46.9	-/-	-/-	2.7/8.3
Gravesend	(16,633)	48.6	26.5/54.5	7.6/15.6	7.2/14.7	6.4/13.2	0.8/1.7
Great Yarmouth	(30,879)	56.0	27.4/48.8	19.2/34.2	3.6/6.7	4.0/7.1	-/-
Halifax	(33,582)	41.4	23.4/56.8	17.1/41.4	-/-	0.9/2.1	-/-
Huddersfield	(30,882)	59.6	25.9/43.4	18.9/31.8	9.0/15.1	1.2/2.1	2.2/3.8
Hull	(84,690)	49.6	15.4/31.0	19.0/38.3	7.5/15.2	1.3/2.6	2.4/4.9
Ipswich	(32,914)	71.2	40.8/57.3	4.0/5.6	8.5/12.0	13.5/19.0	1.2/1.7
Kidderminster	(18.462)	53.6	29.7/55.4	12.2/22.8	4.5/8.4	2.2/4.1	2.4/4.5
King's Lynn	(19,355)	51.9	22.6/43.5	15.7/30.2	4.8/10.0	7.0/13.5	1.0/2.0
Leeds	(172,270)	47.4	16.4/34.5	19.8/41.9	3.5/7.4	2.7/5.6	2.9/6.1
Leicester	(60,584)	62.3	28.0/44.9	9.8/15.7	4.8/7.8	14.6/23.5	2.2/3.5
Liverpool	(375,955)	45.2	18.4/40.7	6.0/13.2	1.9/4.3	1.1/2.4	14.7/32.5
Macclesfield	(39,048)	44.0	20.0/45.4	12.9/29.2	2.8/6.5	1.4/3.1	4.7/10.9
Maidstone	(20,740)	60.8	38.2/62.8	9.8/16.0	3.3/5.5	8.0/13.2	-/-
Manchester	(303,382)	34.7	11.9/34.4	7.0/20.2	3.1/8.8	1.3/3.8	8.1/23.3
Merthyr Tydfil	(63,080)	88.5	5.3/6.0	16.8/18.7	27.1/30.6	32.6/36.8	3.8/4.3
Newcastle-upon-Tyne	(87,784)	40.0	16.8/42.0	7.6/19.0	1.5/3.8	2.1/5.3	5.6/13.9
Newport	(19,323)	59.2	11.0/18.6	12.7/21.4	9.8/16.5	10.7/18.0	11.4/19.2
Northampton	(26,657)	63.4	24.5/38.6	11.1/17.4	9.4/14.8	13.9/22.0	-/-
Norwich	(68,195)	46.1	22.1/48.0	6.2/13.5	4.4/9.5	6.6/14.4	0.4/0.8
Nottingham	(57,407)	57.7	17.8/30.8	15.5/26.8	6.3/11.0	8.9/15.5	4.1/7.0
Oldham	(52,820)	31.7	11.7/37.0	8.4/26.7	6.5/20.5	2.1/6.7	1.5/4.8
Oxford	(27,843)	59.3	40.5/68.3	6.1/10.4	3.8/6.4	7.6/12.9	0.2/0.3
Pymouth	(52,221)	55.1	24.5/44.5	7.5/13.7	5.8/10.5	2.8/5.1	-/-
Preston	(69,542)	25.5	5.2/20.4	6.4/25.2	2.6/10.3	1.0/4.1	9.1/35.8
Reading	(21,456)	68.5	35.4/51.7	7.8/11.4	14.4/21.0	8.0/11.6	1.7/2.4
Rochdale	(29,195)	49.8	10.4/21.0	23.8/47.9	4.1/8.2	6.6/13.2	2.3/4.6
Salford	(63,850)	36.6	15.5/42.4	6.9/18.9	5.7/15.5	1.6/4.4	5.6/15.4
Sheffield	(135,310)	32.1	11.0/34.3	10.9/34.1	3.4/10.5	1.7/5.4	3.0/9.2
Southampton	(35,305)	61.1	33.7/55.2	6.5/10.6	11.1/18.2	2.6/4.2	2.2/3.7
South Shields	(28,974)	46.2	14.6/31.5	18.5/40.0	2.4/5.2	2.1/4.6	1.9/4.0
Stockport	(53,835)	42.8	15.4/36.0	14.2/33.2	6.2/14.4	1.5/3.6	3.7/8.7
Stoke-on-Trent	(53,835)	40.9	12.9/31.6	21.8/53.2	2.6/6.4	0.9/2.1	2.0/5.0
Sunderland	(84,027)	48.5	14.2/29.2	20.1/41.4	4.6/9.5	3.8/7.8	1.5/3.1
Swansea	(31,461)	58.4	11.0/18.8	18.3/31.4	13.4/23.0	11.3/19.4	1.9/3.3
Tynemouth	(29,170)	44.1	17.1/38.9	16.0/36.3	4.1/9.2	1.6/3.7	-/-
Wakefield	(22,065)	71.1	32.3/49.6	19.9/28.0	9.6/13.5	1.9/2.7	2.1/2.9
Walsall	(25,680)	43.3	18.0/41.6	10.8/24.8	2.7/6.3	1.5/3.5	7.4/17.1
Warrington	(22,894)	59.1	31.2/54.5	18.1/30.6	1.2/2.0	1.0/1.8	4.9/8.3
Wigan	(31,941)	53.2	24.5/46.1	5.5/10.4	6.0/11.3	1.8/3.5	15.2/28.2
Wolverhampton	(119,748)	53.1	19.2/36.2	22.5/42.4	3.2/6.0	3.7/7.0	3.7/7.0
Worcester	(27,528)	66.2	46.5/70.3	9.9/14.9	2.8/4.3	2.7/4.1	2.5/3.8
York	(36,303)	62.3	26.9/43.2	19.8/31.8	6.7/10.7	-/-	6.6/10.5

NOTES on the TABLES

IA and PS: See p. 6 above for details of the index of attendance and the percentage share.

Methodists and Baptists: In the above tables the attendances of all the Methodist denominations (whether Wesleyan or otherwise) are aggregated. The same has been done with all the Baptist denominations.

Presbyterianism: Small denominations like the Unitarians and the Quakers have been omitted, but some attention to Presbyterianism is required because of its pronounced concentration in the North East. Northumberland (9.6/22.8). Cumberland (1.9/5.0) and Durham (1.6/3.8) returned about half the national total of Presbyterian attendances (0.4/0.7 corrected) between them. The towns with the largest concentrations of Presbyterians were Newcastle (5.0/12.4), South Shields (5.3/11.4), Tynemouth (4.4/9.9), Sunderland (3.9/8.1), Carlisle (2.8/7.9) and Manchester (2.0/5.9).

Plymouth: The category of 'Isolated Congregations' has been omitted, but in the case of Plymouth, where the Brethren apparently declined to identify themselves as a denomination, the category accounted for figures of 12.9/23.4, easily the highest of any town.

Leicester: The entry in Table D is based on the printed figures, but apparently they contain major errors including a significant over-estimate of Anglican attendances. I am grateful to Dr D. M. Thompson for information on Leicester.

Notes and Bibliography

NOTES

1. *Parliamentary Papers,* 1852-3, LXXXIX, Census, 1851: Religious Worship (England and Wales), pp. ccxxxix-ccl. Only Dorset, Essex, Herefordshire, Oxfordshire, Rutland, Suffolk and Sussex among the 43 registration counties (excluding the city of York) retained a majority of Anglican places of worship.
2. *Ibid.*, pp. clxxviii-ix. This source is hereafter cited as Census of Religious Worship.
3. A. D. Gilbert, *Religion and Society in Industrial England. Church, Chapel and Social Change 1740-1914* (1976), pp. 27-9.
4. Olive Anderson, 'The incidence of civil marriage in Victorian England and Wales', *Past & Present,* 69, 1975, discusses both the national trends in marriage forms and the local patterns in parts of the Border and South Wales.
5. See the works listed in the Bibliographical Note for discussion of the Census of Religious Worship. The Census entailed the collection of numbers of worshippers at morning, afternoon and evening services at every identifiable place of worship on 30th March 1851. The printed summary tables give the total numbers for each denomination at each time of day.
6. Anderson, *op cit.*, puts the peak of English regional variation in marriage forms in 1860-80, though Welsh practice diverged most from the English in 1890-1914.
7. Census of Religious Worship, pp. clv-viii.
8. *Parliamentary Papers,* 1852-3, XL, Fourteenth Annual Report of the Registrar-General, pp. 4-5. The regional pattern here was weaker than that for attendances. The Church's share of marriages held up well in most of the strongly Nonconformist counties, though it fell badly in Wales. The highest percentage of Church marriages was 94.0 in non-metropolitan Surrey, the lowest 62.5 in South Wales.
9. Calculated from Census of Religious Worship, pp. clxxxiv-ix and cxcv-ccxxxiv. The county figures are given in Table C.
10. J. C. Atkinson, *Forty Years in a Moorland Parish* (1891).
11. The regionalization in C. B. Fawcett's *Provinces of England* (1919) is discussed by H. Pelling, *Social Geography of British Elections 1885-1910* (1967), pp. 3-4. Gilbert, *op cit.*, esp. p. 101, adopts a slightly different eleven-fold division. The editor's chapter on 'The Farming Regions of England' in *The Agrarian History of England and Wales. Vol. IV, 1500-1640,* ed. J. Thirsk (1967), p. 1 ff., is a valuable discussion of economic regionalization.
12. D. Sylvester, *The Rural Landscape of the Welsh Borderland* (1969), ch. 8, discusses settlement types. See also Thirsk (ed.), *op cit.*, ch. 1 and pp. 409-12 and 463.
13. See J. D. Gay, *The Geography of Religion in England* (1971), p. 270, for a map of the pre-1834 dioceses.
14. Gilbert, *op cit.,* pp. 100-103.
15. The average annual values of livings in each diocese are given in *Parliamentary Papers,* 1836, XL (594), pp. 25-6, Church Patronage. Among the English dioceses Durham, Chester, Carlisle, York and Lichfield had the highest proportion of populous parishes requiring financial augmentation.
16. On the picture in 1603 see R. G. Usher, *The Reconstruction of the English Church* (1910), vol. 1, pp. 135, 157-9 and 229, and on recusancy over a longer period J. Bossy, *The English Catholic Community 1570-1850* (1975), esp. ch. 5. Puritan worries about the provinces are discussed by J. E. C. Hill, 'Puritanism and "The Dark Corners of the Land"', *Transactions of the Royal Historical Society,* 5th series, 13. 1963.
17. Atkinson, *op cit.,* passim.

18. A. Everitt, 'Nonconformity in Country Parishes' in *Land, Church and People. Essays presented to Professor H. P. R. Finberg*, ed. J. Thirsk (Reading, 1970), pp. 178-99; D. G. Hey. 'The Pattern of Nonconformity in South Yorkshire, 1660-1851', *Northern History*, VIII, 1973, pp. 86-118.
19. J. C. G. Binfield, 'Nonconformity in the Eastern Counties 1840-1885', Cambridge University Ph.D. thesis, 1965, is a valuable treatment, particularly strong on middle-class Congregationalism.
20. R. R Currie's argument in 'A Micro-Theory of Methodist Growth', *Proceedings of the Wesley Historical Society*, XXXVI, 1967, pp. 65-73, that Methodism flourished where the Church was weak and the old Dissent where the Church was strong is much too simple as far as both the regions and the localities are concerned.
21. Census of Religious Worship, Table H., pp. cclxxvi-vii.
22. *Victoria County History, Oxfordshire*, vol. X, pp. 157 ff. and 225 ff.
23. J. Obelkevich, *Religion and Rural Society: South Lindsey 1825-1875* (Oxford, 1976), pp. 7-8, 22 and 46 ff.
24. *V. C. H. Oxfordshire*, II (1907), pp. 218n. and 299; M. Sturge Gretton, *A Corner of the Cotswolds through the Nineteenth Century* (1914), pp. 120-2, 186 and 190 ff.; *Bishop Wilberforce's Visitation Returns for the Archdeaconry of Oxford in the year 1854*, ed. E. P. Baker, Oxfordshire Record Society (1954), pp. 128-30. The Chipping Norton case is discussed by G. Kitson Clark, *Churchmen and the Condition of England 1832-1885* (1973), pp. 249-53. On forest areas see also Thirsk (ed.), *Agrarian History*, pp. 111-2, and B. Greaves, 'An Analysis of the Spread of Methodism in Yorkshire', Leeds University M.A. thesis, 1961, p. 101 ff.
25. *Bishop Wilberforce's Visitation Returns* . . ., p. 7, for Ambrosden. A. Everitt, *The Pattern of Rural Dissent: the Nineteenth Century* (Leicester, 1973), p. 70, table III, shows that in Kent in 1851 70% of parishes with subdivided property contained at least one Dissenting chapel but that only 14% of parishes in single or concentrated ownership did so. The figures for Lindsey were 86% and 18%, for Leicestershire 83% and 27% and for Northamptonshire 77% and 25%.
26. *Bishop Wilberforce's Visitation Returns*, pp. 54 and 72, for Enstone and Heythrop, and *The Diocese of Exeter in 1821: Bishop Carey's Replies to Queries before Visitation*, Vol. II, Devon, ed. M. Cook (Torquay, 1960), Devon & Cornwall Record Society, NS/IV, pp. 48-9, for Chudleigh.
27. R. B. Walker, 'Religious changes in Cheshire, 1750-1850', *Journal of Ecclesiastical History*, 17, 1966, pp. 82-3, notes how morning work on dairy farms hit Anglican attendances and how Methodists could exploit such conditions by providing afternoon or evening services.
28. 'The Sad Fortunes of the Rev. Amos Barton', ch. 1, in *Scenes of Clerical Life* (1858). C. J. Hunt, *The Lead Miners of the Northern Pennines in the eighteenth and nineteenth centuries* (Manchester, 1970), ch. XI, considers the religious developments in a rural area of mining development.
29. By 1821 followers of Joanna Southcott apparently survived only in four small ports in the south-western parts of Devon. (*The Diocese of Exeter in 1821*, II, pp. xvii-xviii.) On Southcott see E. P. Thompson, *The Making of the English Working Class* (1965), pp. 382-8.
30. S. Baring-Gould, *Further Reminiscences* (1925), ch. IV; P. Brendon, *Hawker of Morwenstow* (1975).
31. *Life and Letters of Mandell Creighton, by his Wife* (1904), ch. 6. See Everitt, *op cit.*, pp. 27-32, on market villages.
32. *Bishop Wilberforce's Visitation Returns*, p. 36.
33. See Sibthorp's comment on Lincolnshire labourers in 1863 in J. Fowler, *Richard Waldo Sibthorp: A Biography* (1880), p. 134, and *Bishop Wilberforce's Visitation Returns*, pp. 141-2, on 'large wages' at Stonesfield.
34. *The Diocese of Exeter in 1821*, passim. On the urban contribution to village

Methodism see also J. C. C. Probert, *The Sociology of Cornish Methodism,* Cornish Methodist Historical Association occasional papers no. 8 (1964), p. 38.

35. R. A. Ingram, *The Causes of the Increase of Methodism and Dissension* (1807), pp. 85–6.
36. Greaves, *op cit.*, argues a correlation between non-residence and Methodism in Yorkshire, but Walker, *op cit.*, p. 8, fails to find it in Cheshire.
37. Again Greaves (pp. 41 ff.) sees the tithe issue as a significant factor in the localities, while Walker (loc. cit.) disagrees. W. R. Ward, *Religion and Society in England 1790-1850* (1972), pp. 9-10, 47 and 123–4, and 'The Tithe Question in the early nineteenth century', *Journal of Ecclesiastical History*, 16, 1965, argues that tithe and enclosure weakened the position of the clergy generally without aiding recruitment to Dissent very much in the localities most affected.
38. Calculated from Census of Religious Worship, pp. cclii-cclxxii, with 'mixed and undefined' and 'isolated congregations' counted as a single denomination.
39. *Ibid.*, p. clxi. The increase of total provision for worship (all denominations) had been exceeding the rate of population growth in the large towns since 1821-31. This shows how the Church's response to urban growth lagged behind that of its rivals. The standard study of the work of the Church Building Commissioners is M. H. Port, *Six Hundred New Churches* (1961).
40. These and later calculations are based on the 1851 Census: Parl. Papers, 1852-3, LXXXVIII, pts. I and II, Population: Ages, Civil Condition, Occupations, etc. My figures for Liverpool exclude Reformed Irish Protestants and Jews who added to the city's ethnic and religious mix.
41. The relationship between native and immigrant Catholicism is discussed by Bossy, *op cit.*, pp. 302-8 and 423-7. For the distribution of Catholics in Lancashire see also the maps in Pelling, *op cit.*, pp. xxiii-iv.
42. N. Pevsner, *The Buildings of England, Yorkshire, The West Riding* (1967), p. 234; W. Ashworth, *The Genesis of Modern British Town Planning* (1954), p. 131; E. T. Davies, *Religion in the Industrial Revolution in South Wales* (Cardiff, 1965), pp. 138-9.
43. R. Moss, 'Methodism as a Social Force in the Staffordshire Potteries 1760–1820', Birmingham University B.A. thesis, 1935, pp. 7-8 and 51. According to J. Foster, *Class Struggle and the Industrial Revolution* (1974), pp. 12-3, 21 of the first 42 factory builders in Oldham were definitely Anglican, a low proportion by the standards of the rural aristocracy.
44. In Oldham in the second quarter of the century the Church's attendances equalled only 7.2% of the population, but even after 1837 over 90% of all social groups except large employers used Anglican churches for marriages. (Foster, *op cit.*, p. 130, n. 12, and p. 147.)
45. 'The Church in the West Riding', *Quarterly Review*, 145, 1878, p. 347; *The Church in Manchester. Report of the Bishop of Manchester's Special Commission, 1905-14* (1914), passim. For the 'proprietary interest' of employers, many of them Anglican, in churches, chapels and schools, see P. Joyce, 'The Factory Politics of Lancashire in the later nineteenth century', *Historical Journal*, XVIII, 1975, especially pp. 546 ff.
46. F. B. Smith, *Parsons and Weavers. A Study in Lancashire Clerical Work* (1897), pp. 34-5 and 59. For Lancashire's 'Protestantism' see also J. B. Marsden, *Memoirs of the Life and Labours of the Rev. Hugh Stowell* (1868), and on a later period P. F. Clarke, *Lancashire and the New Liberalism* (Cambridge, 1971), ch. 3. 3.
47. Foster, *op cit.*, p. 130, on Northampton and other towns.
48. R. Newton, *Victorian Exeter* (Leicester, 1968), pp. 76–7.
49. J. W. F. Hill, *Georgian Lincoln* (Cambridge, 1966), p. 297; A. Armstrong, *Stability and Change in an English County Town. A Social Study of York 1801-51* (1974), pp. 73–4.

50. George Orwell, *The Road to Wigan Pier* (1937), Penguin ed., 1962, p. 102. See also the chapter on 'Working Men's Sundays' in [Thomas Wright], *Some Habits and Customs of the Working Classes. By a Journeyman Engineer* (1867), p. 204 ff.; and H. McLeod, *Class and Religion in the late Victorian City* (1974), ch. III.
51. On the differences among middle-class suburbs see McLeod, *op cit.*, and his chapter in G. Crossick (ed.), *The Lower Middle Class in Britain 1870-1914* (1977).
52. F. M. L. Thompson, *Hampstead. Building a Borough 1650-1964* (1974), especially ch. 10, is revealing on the relationship between Anglicanism and estate development in this prosperous district.
53. The picture in York is discussed by Armstrong, *loc. cit.*, and in Bristol by R. M. Goodridge, 'Nineteenth-century Urbanization: Bristol and Marseilles, 1830-1900', in *A Sociological Yearbook of Religion in Britain*, 2, ed. D. Martin (1960), p. 126.
54. O. Chadwick, *The Victorian Church*, pt. II (1970), ch. 5, and Gilbert, *op cit.*, especially p. 145 ff. Increases in confirmations and communicants might, of course, reflect a new style or degree of commitment among existing worshippers rather than a growth in their numbers. They clearly owed something to the increasingly middle-class character of Anglicanism.
55. *The Statistics of Attendance at Public Worship . . .*, tabulated by A. Mearns (1882).
56. *Fact and Figures about the Church of England* (1959), table 29. No figures for Wales are provided here, but see Davies, *op cit.*, p. 185, and K. O. Morgan, *Wales in British Politics 1868-1922* (Cardiff, 1970), pp. 82-4, on the late-Victorian Anglican 'revival' in the principality. See notes 4 and 6 above for Anderson's discussion of 'regionalism' in marriage forms and its decline.

BIBLIOGRAPHY

Works are published in London unless otherwise stated.

The most useful outline works on the nineteenth-century Church of England are Owen Chadwick, *The Victorian Church*, 2 parts (1966 & 1970), and D. Bowen, *The Idea of the Victorian Church* (Montreal, 1968). W. R. Ward, *Religion and Society in England 1790-1850* (1972), is a trenchant treatment of the period of the greatest social and religious ferment. A. D. Gilbert, *Religion and Society in Industrial England. Church, Chapel and Social Change 1740-1914* (1976), is a balanced survey of the changing religious scene. *Facts and Figures about the Church of England* (1959, 1962 and 1965) provides some statistical detail for the nineteenth century and after. R. R. Currie, A. D. Gilbert and L. S. Horsley, *Churches and Churchgoers: Patterns of Church Growth in the British Isles since 1700* (1977), is the fullest statistical treatment of national religious trends but does little to disaggregate the national figures for regions and localities.

The report and tables of the 1851 Census of Religious Worship are contained in a single volume of the *Parliamentary Papers,* 1852-3, LXXXIX, Census, 1851: Religious Worship (England and Wales). The Census is discussed by K. S. Inglis, who pioneered the 'index of attendance' methodology, in 'Patterns of Worship in 1851', *Journal of Ecclesiastical History*, XI, 1960; by W. S. F. Pickering, 'The 1851 religious census – a useless experiment?', *British Journal of Sociology*, 18, 1967; and by D. M. Thompson, 'The 1851 Religious Census: Problems and Possibilities', *Victorian Studies*, XI, 1967-8. Editions of the MS returns of the Census to be published so far are *Bedfordshire Ecclesiastical Census 1851,* ed. D. W. Bushby, in Bedfordshire Historical Record Society, vol. 54, 1975; *Lincolnshire Returns of the Census of Religious Worship 1851,* ed. R. W. Ambler, Lincoln Record Society, vol. 72, 1979; and *The Religious Census of 1851. A Calendar of the Returns Relating to Wales. Vol. I, South Wales,* ed. I. G Jones and D. Williams, Cardiff (1976). The results of the newspaper censuses of the early 1880s were tabulated by A. Mearns, *The Statistics of Attendance at Public Worship, as Published . . . by the Local Press* (1882).

The regionalization of English society is discussed by *The Agrarian History of England and Wales. Vol. IV, 1500-1640,* ed. J. Thirsk (1967); by H. Pelling, *Social Geography of British Elections 1885-1910* (1967); by J. D. Gay, *The Geography of Religion in England* (1971), which makes extensive use of the 1851 Census results and provides helpful maps; and by H. McLeod, 'Class, Community and Region: The Religious Geography of Nineteenth Century England', in *A Sociolcgical Yearbook of Religion in Britain,* 6, ed. M. Hill (1973). O. Anderson, 'The Incidence of Civil Marriage in Victorian England and Wales', *Past & Present,* 69 (1975), studies parts of the northern Border and South Wales as well as the larger regional pattern.

Two indispensable contributions to the religious sociology of the countryside are A. Everitt, *The Pattern of Rural Dissent: The Nineteenth Century* (Leicester, 1973), and the same author's 'Nonconformity in Country Parishes' in *Land, Church and People. Essays presented to Professor H. P. R. Finberg,* ed. J. Thirsk (Reading, 1970). Other works dealing with predominantly rural areas are M. R. Austin, 'The Church of England in the County of Derbyshire 1772-1832', London University PhD Thesis, 1969; C. Binfield, 'Nonconformity in the Eastern Counties, 1840-1885, with reference to its social background', Cambridge University PhD Thesis, 1965; B. Greaves, 'An Analysis of the Spread of Methodism in Yorkshire (1740-1831)', Leeds University M.A. Thesis, 1961; R. M. Goodridge, 'The Religious Condition of the West Country in 1851', *Social Compass,* XIV, 1967, on the Bristol hinterland; D. G. Hey, 'The Pattern of Nonconformity in South Yorkshire, 1660-1851', *Northern History,* VIII, 1973; D. McClatchey, *Oxfordshire Clergy 1777-1869* (Oxford, 1960); J. Obelkevich, *Religion and Rural Society: South Lindsey 1825-1875* (Oxford, 1976); J. C. C. Probert, *The Sociology of Cornish Methodism,* Cornish Methodist Historical Association occasional papers, no. 8 (1964); D. M. Thompson, 'The Churches and Society in Leicestershire, 1851-1881', Cambridge University PhD Thesis, 1969, and his 'The Churches and Society in nineteenth century England: a rural perspective' in *Studies in Church History,* 8, ed. G. J. Cuming and D. Baker (Cambridge, 1972); R. B. Walker, 'Religious Changes in Cheshire, 1750-1850', *Journal of Ecclesiastical History,* 17, 1966; and W. M. Williams, *The Sociology of an English Village: Gosforth* (1964), on a Cumberland village. Three works dealing largely with industrialization outside the large towns are E. T. Davies, *Religion in the Industrial Revolution in South Wales* (Cardiff, 1965); C. J. Hunt, *The Lead Miners of the Northern Pennines in the eighteenth and nineteenth centuries* (Manchester, 1970); and B. Trinder, *The Industrial Revolution in Shropshire* (1973).

For London there are the seven volumes on 'Religious Influences' in Charles Booth's *Life and Labour of the people in London,* 17 vols. (1902-3); R. Mudie Smith (ed.), *The Religious Life of London* (1904), based on the *Daily News* census of 1902-3; H. McLeod, *Class and Religion in the Late Victorian City* (1974), the most comprehensive modern treatment; F. M. L. Thompson, *Hampstead. Building a Borough 1650-1964* (1974); and S. Gilley, 'Catholic Faith of the Irish Slums: London, 1840-70', in H. J. Dyos and M. Wolff (eds.), *The Victorian City: Images and Realities* (1973), vol. 2. For urban Lancashire there are R. B. Walker, 'Religious changes in Liverpool in the nineteenth century', *Journal of Ecclesiastical History,* XIX, 1968; P. Joyce, 'The Factory Politics of Lancashire in the later nineteenth century', *Historical Journal,* XVIII, 1975; J. Lea, 'Baptists and the Working Classes in Mid-Victorian Lancashire', in S. P. Bell (ed.), *Victorian Lancashire* (Newton Abbot, 1974); J. Foster, *Class Struggle and the Industrial Revolution* (1974), which looks at Northampton and South Shields as well as Oldham; and a rather impressionistic chapter in P. F.

Clarke, *Lancashire and the New Liberalism* (Cambridge, 1971). Two works on York, B. Seebohm Rowntree's classic *Poverty. A Study of Town Life* (1901), and A. Armstrong, *Stability and Change in an English County Town. A Social Study of York 1801-51* (1974), have sections on religion. Also worth mentioning are R. M. Goodridge, 'Nineteenth-century Urbanization: Bristol and Marseilles, 1830-1900', in *A Sociological Yearbook of Religion in Britain,* 2, ed. D. Martin (1960); D. E. H. Mole, 'Challenge to the Church: Birmingham, 1815-65', in Dyos and Wolff (eds.), *op cit.,* vol. 2; S. Yeo, 'Religion in Society: a view from a provincial town in the late-nineteenth and early-twentieth centuries', Sussex University D. Phil. Thesis (1971), on Reading; and E. R. Wickham, *Church and People in an Industrial City* (1957), on Sheffield. Discussions of the cities in general include K. S. Inglis, *Churches and the Working Classes in Victorian England* (1963); H. McLeod, 'White Collar Values and the Role of Religion', in G. Crossick (ed.), *The Lower Middle Class in Britain 1870-1914* (1977); J. H. S. Kent, 'The role of religion in the cultural structure of the late Victorian city', *Transactions of the Royal Historical Society,* 5th series, 23, 1973, and the same author's 'Feelings and Festivals: An interpretation of some working-class religious attitudes', in Dyos and Wolff (eds.), *op cit.,* vol. 2.

Valuable material can be found in numerous works of various types which one can hardly list here. Among the important treatments of non-Anglican denominations which have not been mentioned above are J. Bossy, *The English Catholic Community 1570-1850* (1975); R. R. Currie, 'A Micro-Theory of Methodist growth', *Proceedings of the Wesley Historical Society,* XXXVI, 1967; and R. B. Walker, 'The Growth of Wesleyan Methodism in Victorian England and Wales', *Journal of Ecclesiastical History,* 24, 1973. There is important information in many town and county histories, and some of the more recent volumes of the *Victoria County Histories* are especially useful. Anglican visitation returns are a valuable source, and the present author made particular use of *Bishop Wilberforce's Visitation Returns for the Archdeaconry of Oxford in the year 1854,* ed. E. P. Baker, Oxfordshire Record Society (1954), and *The Diocese of Exeter in 1821 Replies to Queries before Bishop Carey's Visitation Returns,* vol. 1, Cornwall, and vol. 2, Devon, ed. M. Cook, Devon and Cornwall Record Society (Torquay, 1958 and 1960). A great deal of local information can be gained from the biographies, autobiographies, memoirs, and published diaries and letters of nineteenth-century clergymen, though as sources they are usually impressionistic, selective and partisan.